Information Duties under the General Data Protection Regulation

JENS NEBEL

ISBN: 979-8-89686-215-4

Staten House

DEDICATION

Dedicated to my loved ones.

.

CONTENTS

1 INTRODUCTION

The protection of natural persons in relation to personal data processing is a fundamental right awarded under Article 8 of the Charter of Fundamental Rights of the European Union[1] (henceforth, the Charter) and Article 16 of the Treaty on the Functioning of the European Union[2] (TFEU). This right is fundamental to the European Union and expressly acknowledged in or implied by the national constitutions of most member states. Specifically, its importance is underpinned by way of its dogmatic construction based on what must be considered the most fundamental human right of all, which is the principle of human dignity.

The Charter requires in Article 8(2) that data be processed fairly for specified purposes and on the basis of the consent of the data subject or some other ground laid down by law. Article 16(2) TFEU calls for the European Parliament and the Council to lay down the rules relating to the protection of individuals with regard to the processing of personal data. According to Article 16(2) TFEU, such legislation is at the same time called to provide for "rules relating to the free movement of such data". This single paragraph alone addresses one of the key issues of any data protection legislation, which is to strike a balance between the rights of individuals concerning their personal data and those of other persons who have an interest in the free movement of such data, which are equally protected as fundamental, such as the freedom to conduct a business (Article 16 of the Charter) or the right to property (Article 17 of the Charter).

[1] Charter of Fundamental Rights of the European Union of 02.10.2000 (2000/C 364/01).

[2] Treaty on the Functioning of the European Union of 26.10.2012 (C 326/49).

The most recent and probably most important piece of legislation concerning the mandate laid down in these articles is the Regulation (EU) 2016/679 of the European Parliament and of the Council of 27.10.2016 on the protection of natural persons with regard to the processing of personal data and on the free movement of such data[3] (the "General Data Protection Regulation" or the "GDPR"), which at the same time repealed the previous Directive 95/46/EC[4] (the "Data Protection Directive" or "DPD"). The GDPR has become effective and replaced the Data Protection Directive on 25. May 2018.

The GDPR stresses the importance of data processing transparency to concerned individuals. This is highlighted by the fact that transparency is prominently named in Article 5(1)(a) GDPR as part of the first principle that must be complied with in the course of any data processing. While transparency as a principle is of a rather general nature, the GDPR elaborates on it in the context of various duties imposed on those persons determining the means and purposes of personal data processing (such persons defined as "controllers" in the GDPR).

In particular, controllers are legally required to provide transparent information to individuals. For example, the controller must provide the individual whose data is going to be processed (defined as the "data subject" in the terminology of the GDPR) an array of information, including the purposes of the processing for which the personal data are intended, as well as the legal basis for such processing (Article 13(1)(c) GDPR), the recipients of the personal data (Article 13(1)(e) GDPR), the period for which the personal data will be stored (Article 13(2)(a) GDPR), or, where the controller intends to further process the personal data for a purpose other than that for which the personal data were originally collected, information on such other purpose (Article 13(3) GDPR).

Where the controller cannot rely on one of the other alternatives of processing lawfulness, they will need to ask for the data subject's consent. Within the context of a consent declaration, the controller must again provide

---

[3] Regulation (EU) 2016/679 of the European Parliament and of the Council of 27.10.2016 on the protection of natural persons with regard to the processing of personal data and on the free movement of such data and repealing Directive 95/46/EC (General Data Protection Regulation), published in the *Official Journal of the European Union* No. L 119/1 on 04.05.2016.

[4] Directive 95/46/EC of the European Parliament and of the Council of 24.10.1995 on the protection of individuals with regard to the processing of personal data and on the free movement of such data, published in the *Official Journal of the European Union* No. L 281/31 on 23.11.1995.

extensive information, while any failure to do so will render the consent declaration invalid (Article 7(2) GDPR).

The GDPR requires any information and communication relating to personal data processing to be concise, easily accessible, and easy to understand (Article 12(1) GDPR). Given that the controller is responsible for and must be able to demonstrate compliance with the transparency principle (Article 5(2) GDPR), any mistake, inconsistency, or choice of improper wording may expose them to severe legal consequences. Most notably, infringements of the transparency principle, violations of the information duties, or processing on a consent declaration which turns out to be invalid due to lack of information will be punishable with administrative fines of up to €20 million or, in the case of an undertaking, up to 4% of the total worldwide annual turnover of the preceding financial year, whichever is the higher.

This unique combination of extensive information duties and severe penalties presents considerable risks to undertakings in Europe, as it may easily turn out to act as a deterrent to the free movement of personal data. This work seeks to address some of the uncertainties connected with information duties and provide a proposal on those provisions' legal interpretation.

2 OBJECTIVES

In the author's practical experience as a legal advisor in the field of data protection law, the uncertainties surrounding information duties continue to present a severe challenge to data controllers in the public and private sector.

Based on how paramount the principle of transparency has been viewed by the lawmaker, the law stresses various information duties and threatens severe punishment if controllers fail to comply. This work seeks thus to tackle a number of frequently discussed issues surrounding the information duties under Articles 13 and 14 GDPR and provide recommendations on how these questions should be legally interpreted. Subsequently, it tries to offer recommendations to businesses on how to implement the information duties with a fair chance of avoiding high fines. Furthermore, it highlights where the legal interpretation leads to results that seem unjustified or that should – de lege ferenda – be refined in a future update of the GDPR.

2.1 Data Protection Information's Required Level of Detail

Among the foremost topics to be discussed in the context of information duties is the level of detail that needs to be applied to data protection information. The GDPR calls for information in a "concise, transparent, intelligible and easily accessible form, using clear and plain language" (Article 12(1) GDPR). This can present a challenge, particularly to those controllers who conduct extensive data processing. Too thorough and detailed information may jeopardize the goals of transparency and intelligibility, as privacy statements may become very long and thus practically unreadable, which poses the following question:

- Should the data protection information be rather less detailed or rather extensive?

2.2 Language and Accessibility

Art. 12 (1) GDPR requires information to be provided in an intelligible form and clear and plain language, particularly when it is addressed to children. With regard to language, the thesis answers the following questions:

- Is a data controller obliged to provide the information in a language that the data subject actually speaks?
- Must the data controller cater for data subjects with disabilities, such as visually impaired persons?

2.3 Time of Information

Various questions arise concerning the point in time when the information needs to be provided. Different cases need to be addressed – in particular, the following:

- When does the information need to be provided if data are obtained directly from the data subject (Art. 13 GDPR)?
- When does the information need to be provided if data are not obtained directly from the data subject (Art. 14 GDPR)?
- When does the information need to be provided in case of a change in the processing purpose?
- When does the information need to be provided if it forms the basis of the data subject's consent?

2.4 Form of Information

It is also questionable in what form the information must be provided. Although Art. 12 (1) (1) GDPR speaks of a precise, transparent, comprehensible, and easily accessible form, despite the use of the term "form", this legal requirement concerns either the language used or the way in which it is made available but not whether the information must be provided in writing, orally, or in another form. Rather, Art. 12 (1) (2) and (3) GDPR provide more detailed information about this question. Specifically, it is to be transmitted "in writing or in another form, possibly also orally" (sentence 2). If requested by the data subject, it may be provided orally, provided that the data subject's identity has been established in another form (sentence 3), which poses the following questions:

- Is the controller required to provide the information in writing?
- Does the information need to be provided electronically?
- Is the oral provision of information sufficient?

2.5 Information's Required Content

A number of core questions also arise concerning the required content of the information, the specific items of which are lined out in Articles 13 and 14 GDPR. The present work discusses the meaning of selected requirements. In particular:

- The controller is required to indicate the purposes of the processing as well as the legal basis. Does the provision of this information create a self-binding effect for the controller, or is the controller eligible to rely on additional purposes or legal bases even if they were not originally contained in the data protection information?
- Is the controller required to name the recipients of personal data, or is it sufficient to name only the recipients' categories?
- Is the controller required to indicate the exact period for which the personal data will be stored, or is it sufficient to indicate the criteria used to determine the storage period?

2.6 Person to Provide the Information

There question arises whether it matters who is to provide the necessary information to the data subject. This question can in turn be subdivided into the following questions:

- Who is under the legal obligation to provide the information under Articles 13 and 14 GDPR?
- Does the obligated party need to provide the information personally, or can they do it through other persons?
- Who is the obligated party in constellations in which more than one person is to be regarded as responsible within the meaning of the GDPR (joint controllership, Art. 26 GDPR)?

2.7 Administrative Fines in Case of Violation

Finally, any violation of the information duties may result for companies in severe administrative fines up to €20 million or up to 4% of the total worldwide annual turnover (whichever is the higher). Article 83 (2) GDPR states that when deciding whether to impose an administrative fine and deciding on the amount, the nature, gravity, and duration of the infringement and the level of damage suffered by data subjects are to be taken into account, which poses the following question:

- Will failure to comply with the information duties be considered a rather major or minor infringement?
- What is the number of administrative fines controllers must usually expect?

3 LITERATURE REVIEW

The review of literature, based on which the objectives of this thesis were pursued, is two-fold:

On the one hand, legal literature exists on the analysis of certain legal requirements as set forth in the law. Given that the scope of legal questions addressed in this work is rather diverse, this work refrains from providing a monolithic literature review in the form of a separate chapter. Instead, as is the norm in legal writing, it cites the respective academic literature in the context of the particular questions in which they are legally discussed.

On the other hand, a relevant amount of research is available on how data subjects perceive data protection information (or, in some studies, other legal texts, such as general terms and conditions). This research is reviewed in the present chapter:

In a report prepared for the Office of the Privacy Commissioner of Canada (Phoenix Strategic Perspectives, 2013), the researchers, after conducting a representative study among Canadians through phone interviews, found that while the participants expressed a high level of concern over their personal privacy (66% expressed significant concern or higher), they rated their knowledge of data protection rights as fairly limited (63% rated it as neutral or low). Most participants (81%) thought that websites ought to inform their users about the use and processing of their personal data. Nevertheless, most Canadians do not consult websites' privacy information (50% do so rarely or never), perhaps because, as reported by the participants, privacy policies lack clarity. In their self-assessment, 68% claimed not to have chosen a particular site at least once due to them being uncomfortable with the privacy terms.

In another experiment by Steinfeld (2016), it was found that when, in the process of registering on a website, the privacy policy is not displayed to users by default, users will usually refrain from clicking on the non-obligatory link to actually access the document. Even when users access the document, they usually spend less time reading it than users to whom the policy's text is mandatorily displayed.

This finding was somehow contradicted by users' self-assessment in another study by Earp et al. (2003), which found that 54% of them claimed that they would read the privacy policy upon their first website visit.

Vail et al. (2008) compared regular paragraph-style policies with more visual variants clearly lining out the privacy goals and vulnerabilities. The authors found that users have a hard time comprehending classical paragraph-style policies even though they consider those policies more trustworthy than the more visual and plain variant.

When testing the degree of users' comprehension of privacy policies, a study by Vu et al. (2016) shows that the comprehension rate was quite low regardless of whether the users were asked to answer a question that had been dealt with in the policy they were given to read before the experiment or had to locate a particular answer to a given question in the privacy policy in front of them.

Other research has found that it does not really matter whether the language in privacy policies is rather vague or explicit when it comes to the degree of comprehension (Strahlihevitz et al., 2016).

The issue is not limited to privacy policies, as it has been established that many consumers do not even read the terms of a contract (e. g., Facebook's end-user license agreement) they are entering (Ayres (2014).

It has been observed that there appears to be a difference between privacy preferences and actual behaviour. Even when users obtain and understand the relevant privacy information, it has been shown in various studies that people still disregard any concerns and readily provide personal data, even when told that such data were expressly not necessary for meeting the website's respective purpose (Spiekermann et al., 2001; Behrendt et al., 2005; Norberg et al., 2007).

It has also been found that the length and visibility of a privacy policy on a website has a significant impact on the perceived importance (Capistrano et al., 2015).

In a study dealing with terms of service (albeit with specific privacy content), it was found that when being sent a confirmation email following signing up for a service, only 2% opened the link to the full text of the terms of service (Kljun et al., 2015).

When it comes to their behaviour, consumers have been found to act inconsistently to their stated preferences and beliefs. Spiekermann et al. (2001)

demonstrated that even participants who assessed themselves as being identity-concerned or even "privacy fundamentalists" were willing to disclose a great degree of personal information, to the extent that a revealing profile could be calculated. This was in sharp contrast to their attitude. The hypothesis that the breadth and depth of personal information a customer was willing to disclose was related to the degree of privacy concerns could not be confirmed.

Another study (Fodor et al., 2015) examined whether the perceived privacy risks influenced the adoption of location-based services (i.e., services that are offered depending on the geolocation of a person, usually determined by using data from the person's cell phone). The authors found that this was not the case, which is perhaps surprising.

A general problem with the transparency principle was examined by Chua et al. (2015) also outside Europe: While organisations are required to provide transparent information, that information must be complete and accurate. It was shown that the readability of a privacy notice (preferable in terms of transparency) had a negative correlation with the degree of compliance with other data protection-related requirements.

In a study conducted by Bergmann (2009) with a casual sample, the fictitious privacy policy of a restaurant was tested. A link to a complete continuous text of the privacy policy was compared with an icon-based variant with links to the policy's various sections. As a result, the users objectively understood the icon-based variant better, while subjectively they could not identify any differences between the two variants according to their self-assessment.

In another study by Carlton (2018), fictitious variants of an online shop's privacy policy were compared within the framework of a casual sample. The users' trust in the provider was queried. If the online shop used a standard privacy policy in continuous text or a layered tabular privacy policy with links to the policy's complete sections, the users' trust in the provider was greater than with a standardised tabular privacy policy with graphic elements.

In a study by Elshout et al. (2016), the fictitious general terms and conditions of a clothing shop were checked regarding the approval rate and comprehension. In addition, users were asked to subjectively assess their trust in the provider, comprehensibility, and satisfaction. General terms and conditions were compared in a short and a long version and in a poorly legible and easily legible version. The users' self-assessment was that they preferred short but easy-to-read general terms and conditions to long, hard-to-read ones. The approval rate was higher for short General Terms and Conditions (GTCs) than for long ones, while readability had no influence on the approval rate. The same was true for the comprehension of the GTCs.

In a representative study aimed at smartphone users, Gerlach et al. (2019) examined the fictitious privacy policy of a personalised mobile messaging app comparing the variants (1) no privacy policy, (2) privacy policy of only two sentences in a neutral style, (3) privacy policy with a length of four sentences written in a rational style, and (4) privacy policy with a length of four sentences written in an emotional style. They found that comprehension was better with variant (4) than with variant (2). The latter led to better comprehension than the longer privacy statement written in a rational style. Unsurprisingly, the lowest level of comprehension was found in variant 1, where no privacy statement was used at all.

Gluck et al. (2016) reviewed the fictitious privacy statement of the health software FitBit in a study conducted with a casual sample. They used privacy statements of different lengths (short, medium, and long). In addition, the privacy statement's "undertone" or framing was changed from negative to neutral to positive. Medium and long privacy statements were better understood than ones. There was no significant difference relative to the selected framing.

Groom et al. (2011) examined fictitious privacy statements of a search engine as part of a random sample. Specifically, they compared variants without a privacy statement, variants with a link reference to a complete privacy statement body text, and variants with a link reference to a tabular privacy statement formulated in simple language. According to users' self-assessment, there was no difference between the different variants relative to the provision of personal information. Objectively, no difference was measured either. However, the display of an interactive avatar increased the amount of perceived information compared to the classic display and subjectively improved the assessment of privacy protection from the users' point of view.

Kelley et al. (2010) anonymised and compared the real privacy statements of four major US corporations and found that structured and highly streamlined privacy statements with and without colour coding enhanced the objective understanding of the content compared to a classic privacy statement in continuous text or a layered tabular privacy statement with a link to the full continuous text. Comprehension questions about the privacy statement could be answered more quickly with the mentioned streamlined variants than with the continuous text variant or the layered tabular variant with a link to the full continuous text. Compared to the classic continuous text, all variants were subjectively rated as more useful from the user's point of view.

In a representative study, Kettner et al. (2018) examined the fictitious privacy policy of a smartphone shop. Specifically, they compared a classic version with continuous text with a structured one-page short version and a structured one-page short version with icons. The reading probability and scrolling depth were higher for the structured one-page versions with and without icons than for the continuous text variant. According to the participants' self-assessment, reading intensity was higher for these two variants. With regard to comprehensibility, information content, completeness, and trust in the provider, however, there was no significant difference between all three variants.

In another study, Kettner et al. (2018) examined the customers of a real-life mail-order company based on the real privacy policy. A classic privacy policy with continuous text was compared to a layered one-page privacy policy short version with links to the full-text sections. Only 0.2% of the customers opened the privacy statement link in the web shop. The reading probability was objectively higher for the layered one-page short version than for the classic continuous text variant. According to the participants' self-assessment, however, there was no difference between the two versions in terms of reading intensity, comprehensibility, information content, completeness, and clarity.

Lee et al. (2013) compared fictitious variants of a hotel's privacy policy with each other. The classic continuous text version was compared to a video with a length of 126 seconds, in which the abridged version of the privacy policy was read out. The time spent on the privacy policy was objectively longer with the video than with the text version. The understanding of the privacy statement also turned out to be better with the video. The participants also rated the privacy protection and trust in the provider higher with the video version than with the continuous text version.

Levy et al. (2008) compared fictitious privacy statements of three US banks. The versions used were a tabular privacy statement, a privacy statement in body text with bullet points, one in body text with all content to be covered by US banks, and one in body text with emphasis on provider-specific relevant content. In the survey, the tabular privacy policy ensured a higher level of understanding of the content. Subjectively, there was no relevant difference from the participants' perspective.

McDonald et al. (2009) compared the real-life privacy statements of six US corporations with each other by contrasting the variants continuous text (1), tabular privacy statement with area-related colour coding of the data protection level (2), and a layered privacy statement with links to the complete privacy statement sections (3). The time taken to process comprehension questions on the privacy statement was objectively longer for the continuous text variant than for the other two variants. The tabular privacy statement with colour coding ensured a better understanding of the privacy statement. However, regardless of the format, the level of basic understanding for all questions that required the information to be processed in terms of content was low. According to the users' assessment, the tabular privacy statement with colour markings inspired greater trust in the provider's privacy protection, whereas there was no difference in the ability to find relevant information and satisfaction with the privacy statement.

Pan et al. (2006) examined the fictitious privacy policy of a gift shop was by comparing a privacy policy in body text with almost 2,000 words, which was drafted in highly technical legal language, with a more simply formulated privacy policy of just under 600 words in length. The users' self-assessment of readability, comprehensibility and complexity was higher for the shorter and more straightforward privacy policy. In contrast, users rated the first variant's clarity as higher. According to the participants' self-assessment, there was no difference between the two variants in terms of trust in the provider.

Plaut et al. (2012) examined a music shop's fictitious terms of use in both a continuous text variant and an articulated list with five chapters. In the structured list, users' dwell time was objectively higher, as were comprehension and probability of agreement.

Reeder et al. (2008) assessed a US publisher' real privacy policy in anonymised form. Variants in continuous text and in layered tabular presentation with visual elements were compared. The time required to answer comprehension questions was longer with the layered tabular privacy policy than with the plain text. Comprehension was also higher with the continuous text, as was satisfaction with the privacy statement according to the participants' self-assessment.

Soumelidou et al. (2020) examined Instagram's real privacy policy. Three variants were compared, namely an articulated continuous text, a layered text articulated or visualised with keywords or ICONs, and a layered privacy policy visualised with networked clouds. The participants rated the privacy protection by Instagram higher for the two graphical variants than for the purely structured continuous text.

4 METHODOLOGY

This work employed a standard legal methodological approach including an analysis of data:

4.1 Standard Legal Methodology

As far as the legal interpretation of the GDPR is concerned, this work generally made use of the standard legal methodology in the interpretation of statutory law. The European Court of Justice established that a uniform application of community law and the principle of equality require that the terms of a provision of community law for the purpose of determining its meaning and scope must normally be given an independent and uniform interpretation throughout the community, taking into account the context of the provision and the purpose of the relevant regulations.[5] To this end, this work offers an interpretation of the respective provisions following a grammatical, systematic, historical, and teleological analysis (Stotz, 2015, p. 495 et seq.).

4.2 Specific Attention to the *Effet Utile* principle

However specific the legal questions, the GDPR operates under the general assumption that transparent information is crucial for users to exercise their right to data protection, particularly on the internet: The concept of consent entirely relies on the presupposition that data subjects shall have control over the processing of their personal data and will determine whether they give their

[5] Judgment of the ECJ of 18.01.1984, Case 327/82 (Ekro), ECR 1984, 107.

consent according to the associated benefits and disadvantages that are either expressly presented or otherwise recognizable to them.

For instance, the lawmaker expects that when given the choice between two similar offerings in terms of quality and price, the data subject as a consumer would opt for the offer where, according to their level of knowledge, either they are not required to give their consent or the offering encompasses less personal data processing.

This does have drawbacks on the legal interpretation because European law is to be interpreted based on an *effet utile* approach: The European Court of Justice often relies on this principle,[6] which, in essence, entails that the interpretation is intended to give the most practical effect to the respective provision (Riesenhuber, 2015, p. 217). This in turn poses the question of what practical effect data protection information usually has.

4.3 Deriving Numbers for the *Effet Utile* Approach – Part 1

Based on this reasoning and the *effet utile* approach, for the legal analysis, particularly the teleological analysis, it is essential to understand the practical effect of data protection information for data subjects. A practical effect could be inferred if data subjects, in their role as consumers of goods or services, adapt their behaviour according to the data protection information they are provided.

As shown in the literature review, the experiments and surveys do not draw a clear picture. On the one hand, data subjects seem to view data protection information as rather relevant, particularly where studies were based on self-assessment. On the other hand, objective results seem to be rather mixed. Therefore, the approach taken in this work was to measure the number of users who accessed a given website that presented data protection information and compare this number to the overall number of that website's visitors. Based on this ratio, conclusions can be drawn about the *effet utile* argument – namely, it is possible to assess how significant the practical effect of such data information can be.

To this end, this work relies on the fact that the presentation of specific information on websites has been legally required for about 20 years in

[6] See for instance Judgment of the ECJ of 03.09.2009, Case C-489/07 (Messner), ECR 2009, I-7315.

Germany: Since 1997,[7] website providers in Germany have been under the obligation to disclose certain kinds of data protection information to website visitors.

According to Article 5 (1) of the German Telemedia Act[8], providers also have long been required to maintain, in an easily noticeable, directly accessible way, among others, the following information:

- name and address, in case of legal entities as well their legal form, and the names of their legal representatives;
- details regarding the communication facilities to enable a quick electronic communication, including the email address;
- information about their trade registration, including the registration number;
- the VAT identification number.

The aforementioned information can usually be found under the label "imprint" (*Impressum*). Failure to provide a proper imprint is deemed a violation of unfair competition law in Germany. Consequently, it is rare, at present, to find a major German website provider failing to maintain a proper imprint.

Additionally, according to Section 13 (1) of the German Telemedia Act,[9] the website operator must provide information at the beginning of each session about the nature, scope, and purpose of collecting and using personal data and about the processing of such data in countries outside the European Economic Area. The information must be supplied in a generally understandable form and is usually provided under a hyperlink labelled "data protection statement" (*Datenschutzerklärung*) or "privacy policy".

Many website providers measure the number of visits on particular pages, including the page where the privacy notice is displayed, which is usually a separate subpage solely dedicated to that particular content. Most website operators use website analytics software, such as Google Analytics, Adobe Analytics, and Matomo. Such analytics software usually measures specific

---

[7] S 3 (5) and s 6 (1) of the Act on the Regulation of Framework Conditions for Information and Communication Services *(Gesetz zur Regelung der Rahmenbedingungen für Informations- und Kommunikationsdienste)*, Federal Gazette (BGBl.) I, p. 1870.

[8] S. 5 (1) of the Tele Media Act (*Telemediengesetz*) [2007] Federal Gazette (BGBl.) I p. 179, as last amended by Art. 2 of the Act of 1. September 2016 [2016] Federal Gazette (BGBl.) I p. 3352.

[9] Now replaced by Art. 13 GDPR, see Oberlandesgericht (Higher Regional Court) Hamburg (Germany), decision of 10.12.2019, docket no. 15 U 90/19, mn. 2 et seq.; Oberlandesgericht Stuttgart, decision of 27.02.2020, docket no. 2 U 257/19, mn. 26 et seq.; Landgericht (Regional Court) Stuttgart, decision of 20.05.2019, docket no. 35 O 68/18 KfH.

indicators to determine how a particular website is actually used. Among the parameters are page views and unique users.

A page view is defined as an instance of a page being loaded (or reloaded) in a browser. Page views are a metric defined as the total number of pages viewed in a given period of time.[10]

A unique user is defined as an IP address plus a further identifier, such as a cookie or registration ID. The metric is usually measured in a given period of time. While the term implies that one unique user actually equates to one and the same physical person using the website, the metric has shortcomings, as the parameter is only suitable to recognize the same machine accessing a website while failing to take into account that a user may use more than one device or internet provider to access it (e.g., a desktop computer and a smartphone). Hence, it may display a too high number of unique users. Furthermore, it may fail to recognize a returning user where the latter actively suppresses the transmission of the additional identifier (e.g., by deleting the cookies from their computer between visits). Subsequently, the actual number of unique users is lower than the measurement would suggest.

By comparing the number of unique users on the website's starting page and the number of those accessing the imprint page and the data protection information page, it is possible to measure how many users actually access the provided information. To this end, despite its aforementioned shortcomings, the unique user's metric was taken as a basis. However, it needs to be noted that not all users access the website through the starting page but may directly view specific subpages (e.g., by following direct hyperlinks or search engines results or accessing dedicated landing pages). This implies that the actual number of website visitors will in fact be higher, while the unique user metric will display more than the actual number of unique users. It is also worth noting that not every visitor who accesses a given website can be deemed to have thoroughly read the displayed information. However, these inaccuracies, which would have led to an even more unfavourable ratio between the total number of visitors and the ones accessing the data protection information, were ignored.

When a visit was recorded, it was counted as one user who actually accessed and fully recognized the privacy information, although that does not take into account returning visitors to the privacy page and users who did not bother reading the privacy information. The number of visits to the privacy

[10] Definition used by Google Analytics, see https://support.google.com/analytics/answer/6086080?hl=en (last accessed 25.10.2020).

page can be analysed in relation to the total number of visitors on the website in a given time period and will likely provide an indication as to what degree of importance website users actually attach to the privacy information. It would be safe to conclude that a user who shows no interest in the information that is being provided will act independently from the content and form of such information.

To gather the website analysis data, a number of companies and organisations were invited to provide such data, encompassing a 1-year period. To obtain a relevant picture, among the invitees were the following companies:

- the 30 largest publicly listed stock corporations (DAX 30);
- the 30 largest websites according to AGOF Digital Facts[11];
- the 10 largest non-public corporations;
- the 10 most prominent global companies;
- the five most relevant media outlets;
- 10 smaller companies;
- the three largest German football clubs;
- German federal government and the European Commission.

Those companies were asked to provide, for a reference period, the number of unique users and page views on both their home page and their privacy policy subpage.

4.4 Deriving Numbers for the *Effet Utile* Approach – Part 2

Effet utile also has a dimension in the legal consequences that follow from the law's implementation. Particularly concerning the administrative fines questions (Chapter 2.7), it seems worthwhile to determine how violations against Articles 13 and 14 GDPR have actually been handled by the data protection authorities, in particular with regard to the amount of fines that controllers usually have to face for failure to comply with information duties.

While there is no full list available on all fines that have been imposed based on the GDPR throughout the European Union, the "GDPR Enforcement Tracker" website[12] still provides a decent overview. Specifically, it lists fines, including a short reasoning of the fine in English, the number of fines, the supervisory authority that imposed a fine, and a list of infringed provisions. Therefore, it is possible to extract all penalties related to a violation of Articles 13 and 14, determine the amounts, and compare them between the respective supervisory authorities.

---

[11] AGOF (2015).

[12] GDPR Enforcement Tracker (2020).

5 QUANTITATIVE ANALYSIS

5.1 Data Analysis – Part 1

Twenty-one out of 100 invitees provided the requested data, representing, according to the unique user metric, an indicator of the behaviour of roughly 3.2 million different website users. Four of those replies had to be discarded because they contained numbers either too high or invalid (e.g., the total number of unique users on privacy policy subpage was higher than the total number of unique users on the home page).

First, as could be expected, there was a correlation between the number of unique users on the home page and the number of unique users on the privacy policy subpage:

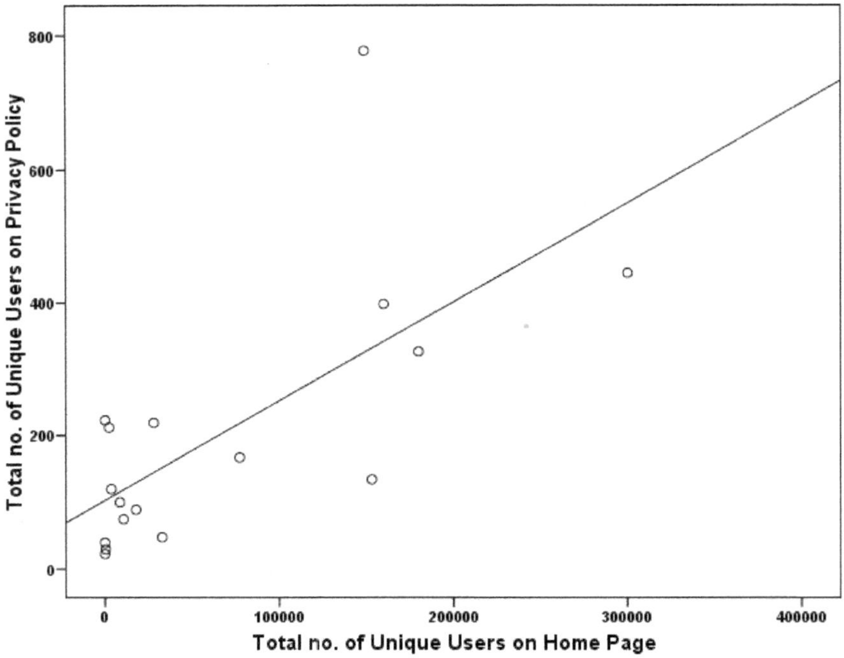

Figure 1: Total no. of Unique Users on Home Page vs Privacy Policy

Specifically, there was a strong positive correlation (Pearson correlation coefficient of .684) between the two variables, meaning that the higher the number of visitors to the home page, the higher the number of visitors to the privacy policy subpage:

		Total no. Unique Users on Home Page	Total no. Unique Users on Privacy Policy Page
Total no. of Unique Users on Home Page	Pearson correlation coefficient	1	.684
	significance (2-tailed)		0.002
	N	17	17
Total no. of Unique Users on Privacy Policy Page	Pearson correlation coefficient	.684	1
	significance (2-tailed)	0.002	
	N	17	17

Table 1: Correlation Between Unique Users on Home Page and Privacy Policy Page

What is striking is that the ratio between the total number of visitors on the home page and the number of visitors on the privacy policy subpage is remarkably low. The results show that based on a unique user metric, an average of about 66,000 users visited the home page in the reference period, while only about 200 of them visited the privacy policy subpage, amounting to a ratio of only .3%.

A similarly low number can be shown based on the median, where the percentage of users accessing the privacy policy subpage is only slightly higher than the average at about .75%:

		Total no. Unique Users on Home Page	Total no. Unique User on Privacy Policy Page	Total no. Unique User on Imprint Page
N	Valid	17	17	17
	Invalid	4	4	4
Average	66,132.16		201.53	2,080.47
Median	17,854.00		134.00	322.00
Standard Deviation	89,364.93		194.90	3,359.27
Minimum	220		23	20
Maximum	300,089		777	10,134

Table 2: Total no. Unique Users on Home Page, Privacy Policy Page, and Imprint Page

There is also a significant difference between the percentage of users accessing the privacy policy and that of those accessing the so-called imprint (a subpage disclosing basic information about the provider's identity, such as a company's address, name, company, and registry no.). The imprint apparently draws a somewhat greater interest, with a ratio of 3.1% based on average and 1.8% based on the median value. The number of users accessing the imprint was thus up to six times higher than the number of users accessing the privacy policy (Nebel 2018).

5.2 Data Analysis – Part 2

The GDPR Enforcement Tracker website[13] lists a total of 429 fine cases, 45 of which are fully or partly related to a violation of Article 13 or 14 GDPR or both:

[13] GDPR Enforcement Tracker (2020).

Country	Fine Amount (in €)	Art. 13/14 GDPR was Primary Violation?	Enforcement Tracker ID (ETID)[14]
Austria	4,800	Yes	1
Austria	1,800	No	2
Austria	2,200	No	4
France	50,000,000	No	23
Hungary	3,200	No	35
Hungary	3,200	No	37
Poland	220,000	Yes	43
France	20,000	No	51
Hungary	92,146	No	61
Greece	150,000	No	65
Romania	2,500	Yes	66
Austria	50,000	Yes	68
Portugal	2,000	Yes	77
Spain	900	Yes	103
Spain	900	Yes	105
Portugal	2,000	Yes	108
France	500,000	No	118
Spain	1,500	Yes	142
Spain	1,600	Yes	147
Hungary	1,430	No	157
Belgium	15,000	Yes	169
Spain	1,500	Yes	208
Spain	1,800	Yes	220
Spain	3,200	Yes	245
Spain	2,000	Yes	246
Spain	6,000	Yes	247
Hungary	4,290	No	257
Hungary	1,715	Yes	258
Hungary	2,860	No	259
Finland	100,000	No	279
Spain	540	Yes	286

[14] All cases can be directly accessed by inserting the ID number instead of "[ID]" into the website address (without brackets) https://www.enforcementtracker.com/ETID-[ID] (e.g., https://enforcementtracker.com/ETID-12 for accessing the case with the ETID no. 12).

Spain	3,000	Yes	298
Spain	2,000	No	308
Spain	2,000	No	309
Spain	1,500	Yes	347
France	250,000	No	362
Spain	3,000	Yes	364
Spain	3,000	Yes	369
Spain	3,000	Yes	371
Italy	15,000	No	374
Belgium	3,000	No	380
Italy	15,000	No	391
Romania	500	No	395
Italy	80,000	No	406
Spain	7,800	Yes	426

Table 3: Fines that Have Been Imposed Based on a Violation of Articles 13 and/or 14 GDPR.

As can be seen, there is a remarkably wide spread between the fines that have been imposed. Upon closer look, however, there are a few tendencies which can be seen, as I will illustrate in the following paragraphs.

5.2.1 The Spanish Way

Spain clearly seems to have been the most active supervisory authority when it comes to the imposition of fines for Article 13/14 GDPR violations. Eighteen of the above 45 cases are attributable to the Spanish authorities. Within those 18 cases, the fines seem to oscillate around €2,000–€2,500 (average: €2,513; median: €2,000 €). After singling out the two cases in which the Article 13/14 GDPR violation was not the primary infringement, not much changes (average: €2,578; median: €2,000). It can be inferred that the Spanish authorities seem to apply a moderate standard, which conforms to the findings of this paper. Nonetheless, it must be considered that the Spanish authorities generally seem to act on the rather low end of the scale, with the GDPR Enforcement Tracker lists only one case where Spanish authorities imposed a six-figure fine.

5.2.2 The Overall Picture

In the overall picture, it makes sense to eliminate all fines where the violation of Articles 13 and 14 GDPR was not the primary infringement. In those cases, only a detailed analysis would reveal the role that the infringement of the information duties played in determining the fine amount, which is hard to implement since in some cases, the exact reasoning of the administering authority was not published or posed a language barrier. It can also be assumed that in instances such as the €50 million fine imposed by the French authority CNIL on Google, the violation of information duties only played a minor, albeit hard to assess, role in determining the overall penalty amount.

When merely relying on the cases where the violation of Articles 13 or 14 GDPR played the sole or at least primary role, the average comes out to €14,136. The median is still low at €2,250.

The big gap between average and median is mainly due to one case, in which a six-figure fine was imposed: According to Enforcement Tracker,[15] the Polish fine in the amount of €220,000 was imposed upon a company which processed the data subjects' data obtained from publicly available sources. However, the controller fulfilled the information obligation under Articles 14 (1)-(3) GDPR only in relation to the persons whose email addresses they had at its disposal. For the remaining persons, the company did not send the information through postal service but only presented it on its website. However, the fine was challenged in Court, which cancelled it due to procedural errors. The Polish data protection authority has announced that the fine will be revised in a new administrative procedure. When omitting this case, the average would come down to €5,185 (median: €2,000).

Thus, the Spanish practice is generally confirmed by the practice found elsewhere in the European Union, with the average and median fines being only slightly higher yet still on the low end of the scale, particularly compared to the upper ceiling of possible fines (Nebel 2021).

---

[15] See https://enforcementtracker.com/ETID-43 (last accessed 25.10.2020).

6 ANALYSIS OF LEGAL DISCUSSION

This part examines some of the key questions in the context of information duties under the GDPR. The current state of legal discussion is evaluated in this chapter.

6.1 Level of Detail

First, the general requirements regarding the level of detail shall be examined.

According to Article 12 (1) GDPR, the controller shall take appropriate measures to provide any information referred to in Articles 13 and 14 GDPR and any communication under Articles 15 to 22 and 34 GDPR relating to processing to the data subject in a concise, transparent, intelligible, and easily accessible form.

First, the GDPR requires information to be in a concise form. The next section explains what that means.

From a grammatical standpoint, the term concise seems to imply some aspect of brevity or condensation, which could warrant that a certain degree of detail may be omitted or at least aggregated in favour of a succinct presentation However, legal writers have argued that concise means that the information or communication has a sufficient degree of accuracy and definition (Quaas, 2018, Art. 12 GDPR mn. 17), which could be understood to stand somewhat in opposition to the grammatical understanding. Perhaps, this argument has been primarily raised by German writers because the German language version speaks of präzise information, which would translate as "precise" rather than "concise".

On the other hand, the French concise, the Dutch *beknopte*, the Danish *kortfattet*, the Italian *concise*, the Portuguese *concise*, the Czech *stručným*, and the

Spanish *concise* seem to bear the same connotation. Given that in all other major language versions of the European Union the term resembles the English word "concise" rather than "precise", it can be assumed that the German version was not translated with utmost precision and that no particular consideration needs to be given to the aspect of precision when it comes to determining what a concise form means.

Based on the general meaning of the term, it is important to note that *concise* is defined in the Cambridge Dictionary as "short and clear, expressing what needs to be said without unnecessary words".[16] The word originates from the Latin *concidere*, which means to cut something down.[17] The word's origin emphasizes the interpretation that concise information is something that is reduced to the essence. Even more revealing is the definition of the Real Academia Española, which defines the term *concisión* as "brevedad y economía de medios en el modo de expresar un concepto con exactitude",[18] emphasizing that this particular mode of expression takes into account the economy of means.

The grammatical interpretation, therefore, reveals an understanding that would favour brevity and understandability over precision in the last small details (Nebel 2019).

Apart from grammatical considerations, how the concision requirement fits into the systematic approach of the GDPR is of great importance for the interpretation. The aspect of concision forms part of the transparency principle, which is stressed in the GDPR in many aspects. Besides being part of the general principles lined out in Article 5 GDPR, it has been given prominent attention in Article 12, which precedes all specific provisions dealing with the data subject's rights. According to Article 12, the requirement shall apply to any information and communication by the data controller towards the data subject. The requirement forms a bracket and connector between all instruments which would necessitate a notification to the data subject.

Furthermore, from a systematic point of view, there may be different levels of "concise", depending on the specific information or communication duty that is going to be addressed. For instance, when Article 13 calls for certain information to be provided when personal data is being collected from the data

---

[16] See Cambridge Dictionary, http://dictionary.cambridge.org/de/worterbuch/englisch/concise [last accessed: 09.08.2020].

[17] See PONS Dictionary, http://de.pons.com/übersetzung/latein-deutsch/concidere [last accessed: 09.08.2020].

[18] See Diccionario de la Lengua Española, https://dle.rae.es/concisión [last accessed: 09.08.2020].

subject, there is no further specification as to the level of detail. However, when looking at Article 15 GDPR (right of access by the data subject), the data subject has, among others, the right to obtain a copy of the personal data undergoing processing (Article 15 (3) GDPR). Since a copy of the personal data will usually reveal much greater detail of information, the general "concise" information requirement may encompass a lesser degree of detail.

From a systematic standpoint, there is also a limit as to what extent information or communication may be abbreviated. In Art. 12 (7) GDPR, provision is made for the use of standardised icons, which are supposed to give in an easily visible, intelligible, and clearly legible manner a meaningful overview of the intended processing. Article 12 (7) GDPR states that such icons may be used "in combination" with the information according to Articles 13 and 14 GDPR. It is thus clear that the information is not fully replaceable by icons. Thus, it can be inferred that "concise" information must be more than an icon which only gives a meaningful overview of the processing.

Regulation (EU) No 596/2014 of the European Parliament and of the Council of 16.04.2014 on market abuse (market abuse regulation) presents a definition of information "of precise nature". According to Art. 7 (2) of Regulation 596/2014, information will be deemed to be of a precise nature if it indicates a set of circumstances which exists or may reasonably be expected to come into existence or an event which has occurred or may reasonably be expected to occur, and is specific enough to enable a conclusion to be drawn as to the possible effect of that set of circumstances or event on the prices of the financial instruments or the related derivative financial instrument, the related spot commodity contracts, or the auctioned products based on the emission allowances. In the case of a protracted process that is intended to bring about or that results in particular circumstances or a particular event, those future circumstances or that future event, and also the intermediate steps of that process which are connected with bringing about or resulting in those future circumstances or that future event may be deemed to be precise information. It is rather obvious that this definition can only be understood very narrowly in the particular context of said regulation and cannot reveal anything useful for the interpretation of the term *concise* in the present context (Franck, 2018, Art. 12 GDPR mn. 17). The following section examines the origin of the concision requirement.

According to the original European Commission draft of the GDPR,[19] the transparency requirement has its origin in the Madrid Resolution of the

---

[19] Proposal of the General Data Protection Regulation of 25.1.2012, KOM(2012) 11, p. 9.

International Conference of Data Protection and Privacy Commissioners.[20] As part of an openness principle, that resolution stated that any information to be furnished to the data subject must be provided in an intelligible form, using a clear and plain language. The original draft, however, adopted this formulation and did not contain a requirement of concise information. Following the Committee on Civil Liberties, Justice and Home Affairs (LIBE) vote, the term concise was introduced into the GDPR, although in a slightly different context. According to Article 11 (1) of the unofficial consolidated version of 22 October 2013, the controller shall have concise, transparent, clear and easily accessible policies with regard to the processing of personal data and for the exercise of data subjects' rights. This was confirmed in the first reading of the legislative resolution of 12 March 2014,[21] with the interesting side note that in the German language version, the term concise was translated with the equivalent prägnant (and not the misleading term präzise, as in the final version). In the draft statement of the Council of the European Union of 17 March 2016, the term concise was then connected to the provision of information and communication, which later became Article 12 (1), with nearly verbatim wording.

What becomes clear from the genesis of this requirement is that it was originally meant to address the formulation of a privacy policy and called for privacy policies that were meaningfully short rather than confusingly extensive. When the duty to publish a privacy policy was omitted, *concise* became part of the requirements of the information and communication duties. However, there is no evidence that the legislator sought to intensify information and communication duties.

Concerning the interpretation, what matters is the purpose of the law and what kind of interpretation serves that purpose best. To this end, the Article 29 Working Party has stressed that information and communication should be efficient and succinct.[22] The article specifically mentions the risk of information fatigue (Dix, 2019, Art. 12 GDPR mn. 12; Bäcker, 2018, Art. 12 GDPR mn. 11). It seems that the above interpretation of rather short and aggregated rather than lengthy information would serve the information purposes best, as it avoids or at least reduces the risks associated with the digestion of legal texts. As shown in the literature overview, the longer the

[20] International Conference of Data Protection and Privacy Commissioners (2009).

[21] http://www.europarl.europa.eu/sides/getDoc.do?pubRef=-//EP//TEXT%20TA%20P7-TA-2014-0212%200%20DOC%20XML%20V0//EN.

[22] Article 29 Data Protection Working Party, WP 260 (2016).

privacy policy is, the less likely it is to read through. Moreover, it seems plausible that the low rate of users actually accessing such policy could be due to their expectation of a long text containing much legal jargon. Whether a more condensed text would lead to a higher acceptance rate in the short term may be questionable because the user would not know of the text's length until they access the privacy policy subpage; nevertheless, an interpretation that would facilitate shorter texts would favour changing the privacy policy landscape in the medium or long term.

When it comes to the "concise" requirement, it must also be kept in mind that the GDPR, apart from protecting personal data, refrains from restricting their free movement (Article 1 (3) GDPR). It is also worth noting that Article 12 (1) does not require the controller to provide concise information at all costs, but only calls for "appropriate measures". This "appropriateness" is mentioned in several provisions of the GDPR, most notably in Article 24 (1), which lays down the controller's responsibility and elaborates on the factors that would have to be considered to determine appropriateness. According to Article 24, the controller must take appropriate measures to the nature, scope, context, and purposes of processing as wells as the risks for the rights and freedoms of natural persons. In this regard, *concise* may mean different things in different contexts. In cases with potentially significant impact on the individual, such as in the context of a credit scoring agency, where an error may severely impair the individual's creditworthiness, information may need to be more detailed (and, to this end, less concise) than in the context of standard data processing activities, such as the processing of employee payroll data by the employer. In any case, the term *appropriate*, in light of the basic freedoms which also the controller enjoys, implies that no unreasonable cost can be imposed upon the controller. To this end, where details would likely not change how an individual would assess the risk associated with a data processing activity, such details can be omitted in favour of a short, quickly digestible text which does not present an unnecessary burden for the controller to produce and update.[23]

It is also worth noting that, at least concerning the information duties in Articles 13 and 14, the privacy notice is not required to state the obvious: According to Articles 13 (4) and 14 (5) (a) GDPR, no information is required insofar as the data subject already has the information. This would call for an interpretation of *concise* that leaves out unnecessary restatements of what can be

[23] On the other hand, the *Verwaltungsgericht* (administrative Court) in Wiesbaden (Germany) has pointed out that in light of particularly intensive data processings, more detailed and explicit information might be necessary; see VG Wiesbaden, decision of 13.05.2020, docket no. 6 K 805/19.WI, mn. 106.

assumed to be common knowledge[24] (e.g., specific details of legal provisions requiring an employer to process and transfer personal data to various tax and social security authorities, as it should be clear to every employee that there exist such duties which an employer cannot evade). Last but not least, the GDPR does not impose a strict duty but only calls for "appropriate measures" to be taken by the data controller.

As the low acceptance rate of online privacy policies shows, customers even hesitate to access such texts, perhaps following previous experience with lengthy legal texts. This thwarts legislators' intention to enable individuals to be aware of the risks associated with both the processing of their data and the exercising of further rights. Hence, information or communication should involve only one step to allow the individual to exercise their rights. For instance, if information about data processing according to Article 13 GDPR only lines out very roughly what data processing activities are taking place, this still enables the individual to demand access to the data (Article 15 GDPR) or make use of other, further-reaching rights. An argument can be made that in light of the consent requirement, the information must only be detailed enough to identify potentially risky activities. If that is the case, individuals may decide whether to make use of additional rights warranted under the GDPR.

As far as the term *form* is concerned, the purposes of the GDPR cannot be achieved if this requirement is interpreted in a strictly formal way. Despite the ambiguous wording, information or communication must be concise not only formally but also contentwise.

The "concise form" in Article 12 GDPR encompasses not only the outer form but also the content of the information or communication, and it cannot be interpreted in the sense that completeness in terms of every detail is required. Conversely, unnecessary details may impede a text's purpose to be quickly digestible. Hence, stating obvious facts can be omitted. As a guideline, the text should be detailed enough to roughly assess the risk associated with the data processing activity, thus enabling the individual to decide whether they want to exercise additional rights under the GDPR.

The GDPR requires information to be in a transparent form, the features of which are explained in the following subsections.

From a grammatical standpoint, the term transparent implies, according to the Oxford Dictionary, that something is easy to perceive or detect. The

---

[24] Or, with the words of the *Amtsgericht* (district Court; Westerstede; Germany), can be drawn from the information "from the perspective of a reasonable and unbiased third party"; see AG Westerstede, decision of 30.12.2019, docket no. 27 C 660/19, mn. 19.

Duden definition of the German equivalent nachvollziehbar adds to this the aspect that something should be traceable. From the word's Latin origin, transparency calls for something to "shine through".

As noted above, the concept of transparency seems to be of paramount importance in the GDPR, as it is highlighted as part of the first general data processing principle in Article 5 (1) (a).

What appears to be somewhat ambiguous is, however, that recital 58 GDPR states that the "principle of transparency requires that any information addressed to the public or to the data subject be concise, easily accessible and easy to understand, and that clear and plain language and, additionally, where appropriate, visualisation be used". According to this definition, the principle of transparency seems to be an umbrella term for the formal requirements (concise, easily accessible, easy to understand, clear, and plain language). However, in Article 12 (1), reference is made to a "transparent form"; namely, there, transparency is only part of the list of the formal properties a piece of information or communication is required to have. While the wording in Article 12 could be an indication that a transparent form has a distinguishable, separate meaning (as opposed to transparency as a principle), it seems hard to track down what that separate meaning could possibly be, given that the principle of transparency mandates a transparent form and vice versa. Hence, from a systematic point of view, it seems as if the mentioning of a "transparent form" in Article 12 (1) is not much more than a redactional glitch, whereas the definition in recital 58 appears to contain every aspect that could render a piece of information or communication "transparent".

As lined out above, the transparency concept was part of the Madrid Resolution of the International Conference of Data Protection and Privacy Commissioners and became a prominent feature of the first GDPR draft.

In the course of the debate, the purpose of transparency was further elaborated in the Committee on Civil Liberties, Justice and Home Affairs. In the draft report on the GDPR by the LIBE committee, it was stated: "The right to the protection of personal data is based on the right of the data subject to exert the control over the personal data that are being processed. To this end, the data subject should be granted clear and unambiguous rights to the provision of transparent, clear and easily understandable information regarding the processing of his or her personal data, the right of access, rectification and erasure of their personal data, the right to data portability and the right to object to profiling".[25] This statement makes it clear that the purpose of transparency

[25] https://www.uni-muenster.de/Jura.itm/hoeren/itm/wp-content/uploads/DRAFT_REPORT.pdf.

is to enable the individual to exert control over the processing of their personal data by way of the rights afforded by the GDPR.

The above finding that transparency is rather a general umbrella term rather than a specific requirement of its own is supported by the Article 29 Working Group, which treats "concise and transparent" as one requirement and does not differentiate between the two terms.26 The arguments put forward in view of the "concise" form to equally apply the "transparent" form.

Transparency could be impaired by an information overflow. It has long been established that consumers, particularly when navigating the internet, are primarily concerned with filtering from the vast amount of information the parts that are relevant to them. A privacy notice or communication which, while complete, buries all relevant information in large amounts of text will not serve its purpose of informing the individual of the core facts that they need in order to decide on whether additional measures, such as the exercise of rights, they deem necessary in light of a particular data processing activity. To this end, transparency can also be understood as a call to avoid "too much" information.

While transparency can mean a reduction of information, it does not warrant that the relevant aspects may be hidden behind nebulous or obscure wording (Quaas, 2017, Art. 12 GDPR mn. 14). The *European Union Agency for Fundamental Rights*[27] views transparency as part of the fairness principle. Any person should be able to establish the existence of data processing files, the purpose of the processing, and the controller's identity.

According to Art. 5 (1) (a) GDPR, personal data shall be processed lawfully, fairly, and in a transparent manner. Herbst (2018, Art. 5 mn. 15) points out that this principle was already present in recital 38 of the DPD, the GDPR's predecessor, and that it meant that in order for the processing to be fair, the individual ought to be in the position to learn of the existence of a processing operation and, where data were collected from him, ought to be given accurate and full information in light of the circumstances. This would lead one to assume that the transparency requirement was a feature of the fairness principle. However, Herbst questions this in light of the Police and Criminal Justice Data Protection Directive (PCJ DPD)[28], which, in its Art. 5 (1) (a), mirrors the

[26] Article 29 Data Protection Working Party, WP 260 (2016).

[27] European Union Agency for Fundamental Rights (2014), p. 95.

[28] DIRECTIVE (EU) 2016/680 OF THE EUROPEAN PARLIAMENT AND OF THE COUNCIL of 27 April 2016 on the protection of natural persons with regard to the processing of personal data by competent authorities for the purposes of the prevention, investigation, detection or prosecution of criminal offences or

wording of the GDPR, with the notable exception of the transparency principle: According to Art. 5 (1) (a) PCJ DPD, the processing must "only" be lawful and fair, from which Herbst concludes that the fairness principle does not necessarily embody the transparency of the processing.

Frenzel (2018, Art. 5 mn. 21) points out that, based on the German-language version of the GDPR (*nachvollziehbar*, which in German can mean "traceable"), one could be led to believe that the transparency principle would only require that the data subject can retrospectively understand how their personal data were processed. However, transparency always includes a prospective element. Accordingly, Frenzel argues, transparency must enable the individual to make an informed decision (for or against the protection of their data). He also emphasizes that the transparency principle requires to make apparent who, when, how, and for what purposes personal data are being processed.

Pötters (2017, Art. 5 mn. 11) refers to the landmark *Volkszählung* ("census") decision of the German Federal Constitutional Court, in which he sees the basis for the transparency principle. In this 1983 decision[29], which gave data protection law in Germany a constitutional basis, the Federal Constitutional Court held: "*Those who cannot, with sufficient certainty, overlook which information relating to them is known in certain areas of their social environment, and who cannot assess to a certain extent the knowledge of their potential communication partners, may be severely hindered in their freedom to plan or decide in a self-determined way*". Pötters sees this equally applicable to Art. 8 of the Charter: Only the disclosure of data would enable the individual to exercise their rights.

The analysis results in this work seem to confirm that a too wide understanding of the term concise could result in an information overflow that would render any efforts to effectively inform the individual futile. Where legal documents such as privacy policies are rarely read at all, it would seem an unnecessary burden to force extensive information duties upon data controllers. This would call for an interpretation of the term "transparent information" in the sense of very brief information that only highlights the most relevant aspects of the data processing.

---

the execution of criminal penalties, and on the free movement of such data, and repealing Council Framework Decision 2008/977/JHA.

[29] German Federal Constitutional Court (*Bundesverfassungsgericht),* decision of 15.12.1983, docket no. 1 BvR 209/83.

The "transparent" form does not provide much additional insight compared to the "concise" requirement. Essentially, the same yardstick can be applied.

6.2 Language and Accessibility

Art. 12 para. 1 GDPR requires information to be provided in an understandable form and in clear and simple language, particularly when addressed to children. This raises several questions.

First, regarding language, the question arises as to whether a responsible person is obliged to provide the information in a language that the data subject speaks. In this context, it is also necessary to clarify how to deal with data subjects' disabilities – for example, what information must be provided to visually impaired persons.

The wording is based on the comprehensibility of the information, not on whether the information is actually understood, which indicates an objective yardstick which does not depend on the individual data subject but on whether, given the general characteristics of the processing, data subjects are likely to be insufficiently proficient in the national language at the place of processing.

Neither in Art. 12 nor elsewhere in the GDPR do we find any comments on the national language to be used. At best, it could be stated that in view of the far-reaching effects of an obligation to provide information in various foreign languages, it could be expected that explicit provision would have been made if such an obligation was to be imposed on the controller.

In some cases, an obligation to provide information in the national language of the data subject may be derived from Article 41 (4) of the Charter (Dix, 2019, Art. 12 GDPR para. 15), whose Article 41(4) gives every citizen the right to address the institutions of the Union in one of the Union's languages and to be provided with an answer in the same language. However, this applies only to the relationship between citizens and government bodies but cannot be applied in dealings between private bodies. From a systematic legal perspective, what national language the information would have to be provided remains unclear

The DPD does not explicitly specify the national language to be used for information purposes. Neither were such requirements proposed in the legislative procedure for the GDPR so that no indications can be derived from the legislative history in this respect.

A criterion for the necessity of a linguistic adaptation may be derived from the market location principle enshrined in Art. 3 (2) GDPR (Paal et al., 2018,

Art. 12 GDPR mn. 35; Quaas, 2019, Art. 12 GDPR mn. 20; Dix, 2019, Art. 12 GDPR mn. 15). According to this principle, the GDPR applies regardless of the controller's location if the controller offers services within the European Union or observes users' behaviour. Although Art. 3 deals solely with whether the GDPR applies at all (Ennöckl, 2018, Art. 3 mn. 11 et seq.), the question of information obligations, which presuppose the GDPR's applicability, must be separated from this. However, the marketplace principle is a frequently used criterion in European law, for example to determine the applicable law of obligations (Art. 6 Rome I Regulation (EC) 593/2008) or the applicable competition law (Art. 6 (1) Rome II Regulation (EC) 864/2007). The marketplace principle takes account of the objective of achieving the internal market because the principle of territoriality, which otherwise applies in principle, means that a trader would have to respect the law of each Member State in which his activities have an impact. The principle guarantees an appropriate balance between ensuring the necessary legal framework and safeguarding practical manageability. The GDPR also recognises this principle by stipulating in Art. 1 (3) that the free movement of personal data within the Union may neither be restricted nor prohibited.

If the marketplace principle is applied to this question, it could be deduced that an offer must be addressed to a specific language area in order to trigger an obligation to provide information in the respective local language. The provider of a website that is aimed at a specific market (e.g., the Czech Republic) does not have to maintain all possible language versions of the data protection information solely because the website can be accessed from anywhere in the world. This would contradict recital 23, according to which the mere accessibility of a website in the case of non-European providers is even inappropriate to justify the applicability of the GDPR. In the internal market, such a legal consequence would also appear unfair because a provider is legally prevented from technically restricting its offer to deny access to users from other member states. According to the Geoblocking Regulation (EU) 2018/302, every EU citizen has the right to shop in a member state ("shop like a local") under the conditions of a local customer. Thus, if a provider is not allowed to close off its internet offer geographically in relation to the internal market, too strict an application of the language requirement could lead to a situation where each provider of an internet site would have to maintain data protection information in all 23 official languages of the EU. However, this would appear inequitable if one considers that the user voluntarily enters a foreign-language sphere where the entirety of the offer is presented in foreign languages as well.

This may not be the case when a supplier directs his offer towards the users of a specific language area (usually a country), for example by designing the other offer in the national language (insofar as this differs from the language in the supplier's home country), choosing the local law with regard to an obligation to be established, or using the local currency (which, however, cannot normally be an appropriate criterion in the euro area). In such a case, it seems logical and reasonable that data protection information should not be provided in a language that the average addressee of the offer cannot understand. In line with this argument, the *Kammergericht* (the highest regional court of the state of Berlin, Germany) held, with regard to the data processing information provided by the messaging service WhatsApp, that "a consumer [...] does not and cannot expect to be exposed to foreign-language general terms and conditions, namely in the event of a dispute to an extensive, complex set of rules of very, very many clauses [...]. Everyday English may be common, but this does not apply to legal, contractual and commercial English [...]. For this reason, all clauses of this set of rules, as long as they are not translated into German, are to be considered from the outset and, regardless of their actual content as non-transparent and all consumers (apart from those with native English language skills or said technical language skills), are to be unfaithfully discriminated against".[30]

On the other hand, it must be considered that according to the results discussed in Chapter 5.1, most people do not take an interest in the data protection information. Hence, it seems doubtful to impose overly strict language requirements on the controller, given that only a meagre percentage will actually bother reading this information.

As a result, it can be assumed that the information must in principle be provided in the national language of the place where the services associated with the processing are actively offered and directed. An offering objectively directed at a specific national market will usually imply that the data protection information needs to be provided in this market's official language. This must be derived from objective criteria, such as the language in which the offering is presented, the currency which may be used to pay for the service, and the top-level domain under which an offering is being presented. However, only in exceptional circumstances can the controller be expected to provide information in additional languages, as when an offering is specifically directed towards an ethnic minority in a particular country that across the board does not have sufficient proficiency in that country's national language.

[30] Kammergericht, decision of 08.04.2016, docket no. 5 U 156/14, mn. 18.

What efforts a controller must make to make the information accessible for the disabled, such as in the case of visually impaired people is also debatable.

The wording of the law does not provide any further indication as to what "accessible" means other than the comprehensibility of the language. The GDPR does not impose any explicit requirement on the accessibility of information.

Systematically, Art. 12 para. 7 sentence 2 GDPR needs to be taken into account, as, in there, The GDPR provides that information "may" be provided in combination with standardised picture symbols. Sentence 2 requires in such a case that these are machine-readable. Without the GDPR expressly mentioning this, the pictorial symbols' machine-readability should first and foremost enable the symbols to be read out through aids. Machine readability is not defined in the GDPR. According to recital 21 of Directive 2013/37/EU, the data are in a file format structured so that software applications can easily identify, recognise, and extract the concrete data. Following the recently adopted Directive 2019/882 (European Accessibility Act), there will be increased accessibility requirements, such as service providers providing information on more than one sensory channel, commencing 28 June 2025. However, it follows from the necessity of this separate legislation that the GDPR itself does not yet impose any special requirements. The use of machine-readable symbols is not a "must" under the GDPR but a "may" – namely, it lies at the controller's discretion.

The legislation's history itself does not provide any significant indication for the interpretation. Not even the DPD contains any special requirements regarding accessibility. However, recent legislative efforts (as pointed out above) indicate that the GDPR itself does not lay down any special requirement.

In terms of purpose, it should also be noted with regard to accessibility that the GDPR does not postulate an absolute standard in this respect, but merely requires "appropriate measures". Specifically, accessibility is certainly not to be demanded in every processing context. It has been argued that controllers should ensure that colours suitable for barrier-free use are employed when designing text. In particular, due to a widespread red-green visual impairment, a corresponding optical design should not be used. In addition, care must be taken to ensure that the text is sufficiently contrasted with the background. In addition, a sufficient font size should be chosen (see Heckmann et al., 2018, Art. 2 GDPR mn. 20). For this purpose, the privacy dashboard model according to the Data Track project may be used (see Raschke et al., 2017). If Art. 12 para. 7 sentence 2 GDPR requires electronic picture symbols' machine-readability, this caveat expresses the idea of not unnecessarily complicating access to information for disabled persons. It does not, however, call for the general use of machine-readable symbols or texts. In this respect, for example, issuing textual data protection notices within a JPEG file would violate the obligation to take appropriate comprehensibility measures. Still, the GDPR does not in any way oblige the controller to provide audio files or machine-readable texts (for such a duty, see Dix, 2019, Art. 12 GDPR mn. 14), for example, in addition to data protection notices in paper form. Furthermore, when data protection information is provided in an electronic (text) format, such formats can usually be processed by aids accessible to visually impaired people (e.g., by way of automatically reading out the text and voice-over functionality).

Usually, when privacy information is provided in text form, this will usually satisfy the "accessibility" test.

6.3 Point in Time When the Information Needs to be Provided

Various questions arise concerning the point in time when the information needs to be provided. Different cases need to be addressed, in particular with regard to (i) information according to Art. 13 GDPR, (ii) information according to Art. 14 GDPR, (iii) information associated with a change of the processing purpose, and (iv) information concerning the data subject's consent.

According to Art. 13 para. 1 and para. 2 GDPR, the information must be provided "at the time of collection" of the data. This raises the questions as to whether a chronological sequence is given, which requires the controller to first provide the information and only afterwards collect data, or whether the data may be collected simultaneously to the provision of information.

The wording "at the time" seems to enable the information's simultaneous provision (Schmidt-Wudy, 2019, Art. 13 GDPR mn. 79; Knyrim, 2018, Art. 13 mn. 11).

This result can be supported by the fact that the GDPR provides a chronological sequence of information elsewhere. A data controller who, at the data subject's request, has restricted the processing pursuant to Art. 18 GDPR, must inform them of any lifting of the restriction before the restriction is lifted (Art. 13 para. 3 GDPR). If such a chronological sequence had also been the purpose of the general duty to provide information pursuant to Art. 13 GDPR, the use of a term such as before or similar would have been to be expected here as well, as provided, for example, in Art. 13 (3) GDPR for the case of a change of purpose.

Sometimes it has been argued, however, that Art. 13 (2) (e) GDPR provided a counter-argument to this notion (see Franck, 2018, Art. 13 GDPR mn. 36). According to the article, the data subject must be informed as to whether the provision of personal data is required by law or by contract or is necessary for the conclusion of a contract, whether the data subject is obliged to provide the personal data, and what the possible consequences of not providing the data would be. Indeed, it has to be acknowledged that this information's primary purpose is to enable the data subject to make an informed decision about the provision of their data. A piece of mere simultaneous information could frustrate this purpose if the data had already been made available at the time of the information.

However, it should be borne in mind that the controller only has to "make available" the information in accordance with Art. 13 para. 2 GDPR at the time of data collection. Whether and to what extent the data subject has already taken note of this information at this time is irrelevant. The information pursuant to Art. 13 (2) (e) GDPR remains meaningful even if data were already collected at the time of actual knowledge because it enables the data subject to assert his data subject rights, such as the right to demand erasure of the data.

The DPD did not explicitly regulate the time at which the information was to be provided (Art. 10).

Already the first draft of the GDPR provided in Art. 14 (4) (a) that the information was to be provided "at the time of the collection". During the legislative process, it was even discussed to what extent the requirement of simultaneous collection and information could be watered down. The proposal, which culminated in the European Parliament's resolution at first reading, provided in this respect for an addition to the effect that the information should be given at the time of the collection "or without undue delay where the above [was] not feasible".[31] Admittedly, this wording did not result in the European legislator's approval. However, there is nothing in the history of legislation to suggest a reverse ranking, which would have made information appear imperative even before the data had been collected.

Some argue that the purpose of the information duties is to ensure that the information – when immediately necessary – must be provided before the data collection begins (Bäcker, 2018, Art. 13 GDPR mn. 56). The information

---

[31] Position of the European Parliament adopted at first reading on 12 March 2014 with a view to the adoption of Regulation (EU) No .../2014 of the European Parliament and of the Council on the protection of individuals with regard to the processing of personal data and on the free movement of such data (Data Protection Basic Regulation; P7_TC1-COD(2012)0011), p. 133.

should enable the data subject to decide whether or not to allow the processing of the data. This view, however, restricts the function of information exclusively to the legal alternative of consent. Nonetheless, the information obligations not only concern the situation of consent but apply regardless of the legal basis of the data processing. It may be true, given the specific requirements for informed consent, that the latter can only be effective if the data subject has the necessary information available in advance. However, this idea cannot be easily extended to the general duty to provide information.

Rather, the information pursuant to Art. 13 GDPR primarily serves the principles of fair and transparent processing (recital 60 GDPR). However, these purposes can also be fulfilled if the necessary information is made available to the data subject at the same time when the collection is carried out. Data processing does not generally present itself as unfair or untransparent solely because the legally prescribed information is not already provided in advance. On the contrary, information that has been provided too far in advance could even damage its own purpose because it can easily be forgotten over time. In this respect, the criterion of simultaneity ensures that the necessary information can be annotated in direct temporal connection with the first provision of the data.

Furthermore, the prior fulfilment of the duty to provide information is not designed as a mandatory precondition for the lawfulness of the processing, unless – in the case of consent – more specific legal requirements exist which make prior information appear mandatory. The GDPR expressly recognises that there may be situations in which the data subject is obliged to provide their data (Art. 13 para. 2 lit. e GDPR). Conversely, the data controller may also be obliged to process data due to legal obligations (Art. 6 para. 1 lit. c GDPR). In any event, in such cases, the lawfulness of the processing of personal data cannot be dependent on the fulfilment of information obligations. If the legislator had wanted to regulate an obligation to provide information in advance, it would at least have had to issue exception provisions regarding the aforementioned case groups of the legally prescribed provision or processing, which, however, do not exist in the GDPR. This also suggests that the fulfilment of information obligations as such can without exception take place at the same time as the collection of personal data.

Again, it also needs to be taken into account that according to the data presented in Chapters 4 and 5, the information rarely plays a significant role for the individual's decision whether or not to allow the collection of data.

As a result, the notion that the information must be provided before the data are collected cannot be upheld against the legal interpretation. To the contrary, there are compelling arguments that the simultaneous provision of the information is sufficient.

In contrast to the data subject collection, Art. 14 GDPR allows a reasonable period of time for information if data is not collected from the data subject. Pursuant to Art. 13 (3) (a) GDPR, the information – taking into account the specific circumstances of the processing – must be provided within a reasonable period of time but, at the latest, within one month. If the data are used for communication with the data subject or are disclosed to a recipient, the information must be provided, at the latest, at the time of the first communication to the data subject or the first disclosure (Art. 14 (3) (b) and (c) GDPR).

This raises the question of the relationship between the provisions in Art. 14 (3) GDPR, namely whether, for example, in the case of an intended disclosure to another recipient, the information must nevertheless be provided within the period set out in letter a (reasonable time limit, maximum one month from receipt of the data) or – if the disclosure takes place much later – only with the first disclosure (letter (c)).

The wording does not indicate any ranking between the different alternatives. The various alternatives are linked by the word "or". This would allow, for example, in the case of intended disclosure (letter (c)), for information to be provided only at the time of disclosure, even if that time should be significantly longer than the period of one month mentioned in letter (a). If it had been the legislator's intention for the three alternatives in paragraph 3 to be understood in the sense of a cumulative application, there would have been no reason to link them with the word "or". Rather, the use of the word "and" would have been appropriate. Hence, according to a grammatical interpretation, it would be sufficient to provide the information in case of an intended disclosure to third parties only with the disclosure or communication and not strictly within one month upon obtaining the data.

From a systematic point of view, neither one interpretation nor the other can be based on decisive indications. Recital 61 of the GDPR also lists the various alternatives to Article 14(3) of the GDPR on an equal footing without mentioning that subparagraph (a) is the basic rule which also applies to the cases under subparagraphs (b) and (c).

However, Art. 14 GDPR contains a graduated concept in contrast to Art. 13 GDPR. While under Art. 13 GDPR, a direct data collection from the data subject always requires simultaneous information, Art. 14 GDPR – in all three alternatives contained in paragraph 3 – assumes subsequent information. Based on this concept, however, nothing can be deduced about the ranking between the various alternatives in paragraph 3. Partial reference (Franck, 2018, Art. 14 mn. 21) is made to the parallel provision in Article 12(1) of Regulation 45/2001/EC.[32] However, this provision also contains the same regulatory construct, without it being possible to infer anything from it for the ranking.

The EU Commission's proposal provides no relevant information as to how the regulation might have been intended. Art. 14 (4) (a) of the draft already contained the ambiguous linguistic "or" construction.[33] It must be mentioned, though, that the first sentence of Article 12(2) of the draft spoke of the fact that the controller had to fulfil his duty to provide information "promptly", which would serve as an argument in favour of a certain obligation to expedite the process. Apart from editorial amendments, this regulatory concept remained essentially unchanged during the legislative process. This could be an albeit weak argument for the interpretation that the earliest of the various alternatives in Art. 14(3) GDPR is relevant for determining when the information according to Art. 14 is to be provided.

Information pursuant to Art. 14 GDPR primarily serves the principles of fair and transparent processing (recital 60 GDPR). Data protection literature unanimously agrees that the earliest possible point in time at which one of the three alternatives of Art. 13 (3) GDPR is fulfilled should be decisive (Dix, 2019, Art. 14 mn. 17; Article 29 Data Protection Working Party, WP 260, 2016, p. 16; Franck, 2018, Art. 14 mn. 21; Bäcker, 2018, Art. 14 mn. 33, 37; Paal et al., 2018, Art. 14 mn. 33; Schmidt-Wudy, 2019, Art. 14 mn. 82 et seq., who classifies lit. b and c as lex specialis to lit. a from which later information could result). In some cases, it is even more strictly assumed that the information must be provided so early that the data subject still has sufficient time to react, and that a time limit must therefore be set for the data subject to submit their point of view (Bäcker, 2018, Art. 14 GDPR mn. 40).

While the latter view finds no support in the law, the question is whether the principles of transparency and fairness actually require a cumulative application of the alternatives in Art. 14(3). The representatives of this view seem to assume that the information in the cases referred to in points (b) and (c) would enable the data subject to prevent the processing in question by asserting one of their rights before the communication or disclosure is

[32] Regulation (EC) No 45/2001 of the European Parliament and of the Council of 18 December 2000 on the protection of individuals with regard to the processing of personal data by the Community institutions and bodies and on the free movement of such data, Official Journal L 008, 12/01/2001, p. 0001 - 0022.

[33] Proposal for a REGULATION OF THE EUROPEAN PARLIAMENT AND OF THE COUNCIL on the protection of individuals with regard to the processing of personal data and on the free movement of such data (General Data Protection Regulation), COM/2012/011 final - 2012/0011 (COD). p. 57.

completed. The Commission considers that the objective of creating such a possibility seems to justify a cumulative understanding of the three alternatives.

However, such a regulatory objective of the GDPR cannot be inferred or derived from the principle of fairness. The GDPR consistently does not recognise any preemptive right of the data subject to be able to prevent intended data processing in advance. This applies regardless of whether the data are collected from the data subject or whether the controller receives them from another source. The maximum times laid down in points (b) and (c) expressly permit information to be provided only at the time when processing is completed. In this respect – even if these are maximum limits which are not meant to be exhausted in every case ("at the latest") – constellations are conceivable in which, for example, the disclosure has already been completed (or can no longer be prevented) when the individual receives the information. If the legislator had wished to implement a different concept, they would have had to provide for a mandatory graduated time–limit model, which – as some have suggested (Bäcker, 2018, Art. 14 GDPR mn. 40) – grants the data subject a prior period in which to comment. Therefore, the information periods provided for in Article 14(3) obviously do not aim to grant the data subject a right of remonstration before the data processing has begun or been completed.

Rather, it is worth taking a closer look at the two specific cases for which the legislator has provided for rules that differ from those in point (a). Specifically, the legislator links the use of the terms "shall be used" (letter b) or "is intended" (letter c) to the legally prescribed purpose of data collection (Art. 5 para. 1 letter b GDPR). By collecting personal data only for predefined purposes and apart from a change of purpose for which specific information obligations exist, point (a) can be understood as a fall-back rule for those cases where data are not collected for the purpose of communicating with the data subject or disclosure to third parties. In such cases, providing for a general rule determining the period within which the information is to be supplied seems justified and necessary. However, where the specific processing situations referred to in points (b) or (c) are present, there is no need to rely on this fall-back position, as those cases can be understood as codified "specific processing circumstances" within the meaning of point (a) for which the legislator has, however, provided for a calculation of time limits different from that provided for in point (a).

If we consider the case provided for in point (b), contacting the data subject using the personal data collected is already foreseen at the data collection stage. In such cases, the focus of the processing is on establishing contact. In this respect, there is a similarity to the case mentioned in Art. 13

GDPR, in which – within the scope of the collection directly from the data subject – a communication situation also exists. In both cases – for Art. 13 GDPR the legislator has expressly regulated this – it is appropriate that the data subject receives the information at the same time[34] as the communication. Moreover, this is in line with Article 13 (2) of the ePrivacy Directive[35], which imposes a similar obligation to provide information in a practically highly significant case of the use of personal data for the purpose of making contact, namely email advertising. In this respect, there are no reasons why, in cases where personal data are collected for the purpose of making contact, information could not be sufficiently provided at the time of making the first contact.

The same applies to the collection for the purpose of disclosure to recipients. Here, too, the focus is on the aspect of disclosure so that it also appears justified that the information only has to be provided at this point in time.

Moreover, in both cases (b) and (c), the legislator has set limits on transparency, as the information should be provided only at the time of initial communication or disclosure and does not need to be repeated in further cases. Hence, the principle of transparency does not necessarily require information before further processing operations.

The legal interpretation provides a strong argument in favour of considering the case alternatives of Art. 14 (3) lit. a - c GDPR as independent of each other. In particular, in the cases referred to in points (b) or (c), the maximum period referred to in point (a) is not applicable.

Pursuant to both Art. 13 and Art. 14 GDPR, if the controller intends to process the personal data for a purpose other than that for which they were originally obtained, they must provide the data subject with the relevant information pursuant to Art. 13 para. 2 GDPR or Art. 14 para. 2 GDPR prior to such processing. In this context, it is questionable whether the information must be provided prior to any further processing (Dix, 2019, Art. 13 GDPR mn. 20) or whether – if several further processing operations for the same modified purpose follow each other – a single piece of information is sufficient.

According to the wording, the information must be provided "prior to that further processing". Accordingly, whether the information is to be

---

[34] See above, Chapter **Error! Reference source not found.**.

[35] Directive 2002/58/EC of the European Parliament and of the Council of 12 July 2002 concerning the processing of personal data and the protection of privacy in the electronic communications sector (Directive on privacy and electronic communications), Official Journal L 201, 31/07/2002 p. 0037 - 0047.

provided only once before the first (further) processing or each time before any additional further processing for a purpose other than the original one remains open.

The general information obligations pursuant to Art. 13 (1) and (2) and Art. 13 (1) and (2) GDPR are also designed as one-off information. In this respect, it is not clear why repeated information should be provided under the merely supplementary provision in paragraph 3.

The draft GDPR did not contain any provision corresponding to Art. 13 (3) or Art. 14 (4) GDPR, which was only included in the GDPR at the Council's instigation.[36] However, the legislative process does not provide any guidance on the interpretation of the question discussed here.

The purpose of the information duty at hand is to ensure, even in the event of a change of purpose, that the data subject receives the additional information relating to that purpose, and it is striking that the obligation to provide information expressly refers only to the information referred to in paragraph 2.[37] In particular, the other purposes, their respective legal basis, or the recipients, apparently, are not the subject matter of the information, as they are regulated in paragraph 1, which paragraph 4 does not refer to. In view of this comparatively limited content of the information to be provided, what would be gained from the data subject's point of view by repeating each individual processing step is not clear. A meaningful interpretation also needs to consider that according to the findings in Chapters 4 and 5, a significantly low percentage of data subjects appear to be interested in the basic information for the original processing purposes. It is hard to imagine why data subjects who do not bother to read the information for the original purpose would be more interested in obtaining the information on additional purposes. In particular, a repetition of this information would not be meaningful either.

As a result, there is no evidence for an understanding that would make it necessary to repeat the information at each further processing. One-time information in case an additional purpose is being used for the data processing would be sufficient in light of this interpretation.

Finally, it must be discussed when the information must be provided if it forms the basis for consent. It should first be pointed out that, strictly speaking,

---

[36] Council of the European Union, Interinstituional File 2012/0011 (COD), document no. 11028/1, p. 101, 103.

[37] Such change of purpose could also result in cases where the controller is obligated to forward personal data to third parties pursuant to a Court order, see *Bundesgerichtshof* (German Federal Supreme Court), decision of 03.04.2019, docket no. VII ZB 59/18, mn 22.

the law does not provide for an explicit duty on the part of the controller to deliver specific pieces of information in the context of consent. Rather, Art. 7 para. 2 sentence 1 GDPR reads as follows: "If the consent of the data subject is given by means of a written declaration which also concerns other facts, the request for consent must be made in an understandable and easily accessible form in clear and simple language so that it can be clearly distinguished from the other facts". Based on this wording, it seems clear that the above standard only applies in the case of consent by written declaration. Since consent pursuant to Art. 4 (11) GDPR is "any unequivocally given expression of intention in the form of a statement or other unambiguous confirmatory act by which the data subject indicates that he or she consents to the processing of personal data concerning him or her", cases of consent given orally or even only by conclusive conduct are therefore excluded.

Even in the case of a written declaration concerning other facts, Art. 7 (2) sentence 1 GDPR merely stipulates that the consent must be clearly distinguishable from the other statements. Specifically, it must be separated from other declarations (e.g., contract declarations) so that it cannot be hidden from the data subject.

More interesting are the requirements regarding the information to be made available to the data subject, as they are unclear. The law only highly generally states that the consent must be given "in informed manner" to be effective. It is questionable what is to be understood by "in an informed manner" in detail and how this requirement relates to the other information obligations, in particular under Art. 13 GDPR.

The data subject must be "informed", regardless of the means and content by which this information takes place. However, the wording points more to the data subject's situation than to the controller's activity so that that consent can be given "in an informed manner". This would apply even if the data subject did not have the necessary information – whatever it may be – through the controller's actions but obtained them through any other conceivable way. In this respect, the law does not contain an explicit obligation to provide information, but the controller will strive, in their own interest to ensure a valid consent, to give out the necessary information to establish the conditions for the validity of the consent. The information must be provided to the data subject in whatever way to make sure the consent is given "in an informed manner".

A systematic analysis of the law does not provide any significant information on the information's timing in the context of consent.

Art. 2 (h) of the DPD already provided that consent should be given "in the knowledge of the facts", which is only another way of phrasing an "informed" consent, and it suggests that the information must be given before consent is given.

According to the meaning and purpose of the provision, one can only speak of informed consent if the data subject already possesses the necessary information at the time of the consent declaration.

The information required for a valid consent needs to be present before or at least at the same time when the consent is declared.

6.4 Form of Information

In what form information should be provided also needs to be discussed. Although Art. 12 (1) sentence 1 GDPR speaks of a concise, transparent, comprehensible, and easily accessible form, despite the use of the term *form*, the requirement concerns either the language used or the way in which it is made available but not whether the information must be provided in writing, orally, or in another form. Rather, Art. 12 (1) sentences 2 and 3 GDPR provide more detailed information about this whereby the information is transmitted "in writing or in another form, possibly also orally" (sentence 2). If requested by the data subject, the information may be provided orally, as long as the data subject's identity has been established in another form (sentence 3).

The wording of sentence 2 first refers to an option for the controller: Writing in this sentence is on an equal footing with other forms. "Where appropriate", the information may also be transmitted electronically, indicating at least a slight limitation. The electronic communication must at least be "given". The use of the term *appropriate* supports the interpretation that this form of communication must be expedient, which would exclude cases where the data subject does not have the electronic means of communication. One could think of the processing of personal data in the course of purely oral communication, such as on the telephone or in a physical shop. In such a case, information can in principle also be provided electronically (e.g., on a website), which would probably also fulfil the requirement of "appropriate" transmission (see also Paal et al., 2018, Art. 12 GDPR Rn. 39; Article 29 Data Protection Working Party, WP 260, 2016, p. 14).

The controller's comparatively wide choice is further restricted based on systematic analysis. In particular, according to sentence 3, the oral provision of information is subject to more stringent requirements, namely that the data subject requested such only oral information. This means that oral information may be sufficient only if it can be attributed to a request by the data subject, whereas processing without such a request requires at least documented information, whether written or electronic (see also Paal et al., 2018, Art. 12 GDPR mn. 38).

The law does not explicitly state the requirements that such a request should meet. However, it will not be possible to impose excessively strict requirements on this, as the law demands an "express" formulation of will by the data subject in other places, such as in Art. 9 (2) (a) GDPR. In Art. 12 (1) sentence 3 GDPR, the "request" must not be an "express" one. It will be possible to deduce from this that oral information does not have to be expressly requested but that such a request can also be made by conclusive conduct.

Conversely, however, it follows from sentence 3 that – as far as the choice between written information and other forms other than oral form are concerned – in principle, the controller may choose what format is appropriate.

Insofar as sentence 3, in the case of information requested only orally, requires that the data subject's identity can be established in another form, this shall not constitute a requirement for the form in which the information is to be provided. The provision of the information must be distinguished from the form of proof of its provision. Pursuant to Art. 5 (2) GDPR, the controller is accountable, namely, they must be able to demonstrate compliance with the principles set out in Art. 5 (1) GDPR. These principles also include transparency of processing (Art. 5 para. 1 lit. a GDPR), which serves the information obligation.

The DPD did not yet contain any provisions on the form of information. Art. 10 of the DPD was solely aimed at ensuring that the data subject "receive[d]" certain information without the DPD laying down rules on the form of this information (this is also pointed out by Paal et al., 2018, Art. 12 GDPR mn. 41).

The Commission's draft also did not yet provide for any rules on the form of information. According to Art. 12 para. 1 sentence 1 of the Commission's draft, the controller alone should determine the procedure by means of which he provides the information. Sentences 2 and 3 in Art. 12 (1) of the current version were inserted at the Council's proposal. The consultation documents show that the question of whether the wording allows freedom of choice for the controller with regard to the form of information has been discussed. The Republic of Ireland argued that it was not convinced that the data subject could in all circumstances claim information in paper form.[38]

[38] Council of the European Union, Interinstituional File 2012/0011 (COD), document no. 9788/15, p. 109.

In this respect, it is hardly possible to obtain indications for the interpretation based on legislative history. At best, it can be stated that the complete freedom of choice, as provided for by the DPD, was restricted to the extent that at least the oral information is now sufficient only under special conditions.

Since the information obligations primarily serve to implement the principle of transparency (Art. 5 para. 1 lit. a GDPR), the question of a formal requirement must be measured by the extent to which the specification of a particular form is necessary to create transparency in the sense of the GDPR. The principle of transparency means first and foremost recognisability which, as such, does not require any particular perpetuation of the information. One could argue that the data subject – especially on the internet – is often confronted with a mass of information that is also volatile – namely, it can be changed or deleted at any time. However, given the law's extensive silence on this matter, whether a hard formal requirement can be derived from the GDPR seems questionable

Art. 13 (4) and Art. 14 (5) GDPR provide an essential indication of the answer to this question. According to these rules, the information obligations do not apply if and to the extent that the data subject already holds the information. Thus, the law clearly points out that the provision of information is not primarily about documenting it but is about making its content accessible to the data subject. Whether and to what extent the data subject considers this information to be so important that they would like to store it permanently is a fundamental decision of the data subject. The controller may, in his own interest and in order to comply with his accountability obligation (Art. 5 para. 2 GDPR), prepare documentation to show that he has complied with his duty to provide information. However, this does not oblige him to transmit it in a particular form. The transparency purpose, in particular, does not require, as is partly advocated, accessibility without media discontinuity (for such a requirement, see Bäcker, 2018, Art. 13 mn. 58.

Ultimately, Art. 12 (1) sentence 3 GDPR also points in this direction because according to this provision, the grant in oral form is permissible at the data subject's request, provided that their identity has been proven in another form. The latter requirement refers to accountability by requiring the controller to demonstrate that they have provided the information to the data subject. However, such a proof should only be necessary to the extent that the controller cannot prove by other means that each individual data subject has received the information, as in the case of a website's users when information is published on that website. Recital 58 of the GDPR points out that information may be made available in electronic form, for example on a website, if it is intended for the public. Pursuant to Art. 11 para. 1 GDPR, the controller is not obliged to collect or store personal data merely to comply with the GDPR if this is not necessary for the actual processing purposes. Hence, the duty to provide information does not require that every single data subject to whom the information has been provided is identifiable (for a general identification requirement, see Kamlah, 2016, Art. 12 GDPR mn. 9; in contrast, see Heckmann et al., 2018, Art. 12 mn. 22, and Article 29 Data Protection Working Party, WP 260, 2016, p. 20).

In principle, the controller has the choice of the form in which to provide the information. Exceptions exist concerning oral provision, which is only permissible if requested by the data subject. However, it usually is sufficient for this purpose if the data subject orally requests the controller's activity, which involves a processing operation and thus impliedly demands the provision of the necessary information orally.

In principle, information may also be provided electronically. This shall not apply only if it appears inappropriate, as when there are reasonable grounds to believe that the data subject is not using the electronic means of communication. As a rule, however, and given the present widespread use of the internet, providing information on a website it should be justifiable, and the existence of that information can also be pointed out to the data subject by other means (e.g., by billposting, in a letter, and orally).

6.5 The Required Content of Information

A number of core questions arise with regard to the required content of the information, the specific items of which are lined out in Articles 13 and 14 GDPR. In this work, the meaning of selected requirements is discussed with a focus on the following points:

- the purposes of the processing for which the personal data are intended and the legal basis for the processing (Art. 13 para. 1 point (c) and Art. 14 para. 1 point (c) GDPR;
- the recipients or categories of recipients of the personal data, if any (Art. 13 para. 1 point (e) and Art. 14 para. 1 point (e) GDPR);
- the period for which the personal data will be stored or, if that is not possible, the criteria used to determine that period (Art. 13 para. 2 point (a) and Art. 14 para. 2 point (a) GDPR).

According to Art. 13 (1) (c) GDPR, the controller must indicate the purposes for which personal data are to be processed and the legal basis for the processing. Art. 13 GDPR concerns the case in which data are directly collected from the data subject. Art. 14 (1) (c) GDPR provides for identical information content in the event that data are not collected from the data subject.

In this context, in addition to the necessary level of detail, the question arises to what extent the information once provided creates a self-obligation on the part of the controller, namely whether the controller can invoke other or supplementary legal bases or purposes even if, for instance, he has not stated them in the context of the information.

A self-obligation could initially be considered with regard to the processing's legal basis.

The wording of Art. 13 (1) (c) or Art. 14 (1) (c) GDPR does not provide for such an explicit self-obligation. The regulations deal exclusively with information duties, while the processing's lawfulness is regulated elsewhere (in particular, in the Art. 6 and 9 GDPR).

For the same reason, systematically, there is a clear separation between the question of information and that of processing' lawfulness, which includes the question of recourse to legal bases. Furthermore, the admissibility rules of the Art. 6 and 9 GDPR contain no reference to a possible link between questions of legality and given information.

However, both questions are possibly bracketed by the transparency principle anchored in Art. 5 (1) (a) GDPR because, on the one hand, it is declared that it forms the basis of the information obligations and, on the other hand, it establishes – at least possibly – a condition of admissibility for the processing of personal data. If this were to be assumed, the indication of a false legal basis or the omission of a valid legal basis could lead to the conclusion that processing which would be prima facie lawful was unlawful solely because of incorrect information.

There was no obligation to indicate the legal basis of the processing in the DPD, nor was such a duty planned in the original commission draft of the GDPR. The duty was only introduced at the Council's initiative.39 However, it follows that the indication of the legal basis was not initially regarded as such a mandatory expression of the principle of transparency. With its draft of the GDPR, the Commission assumed that the transparency principle could be realised even if the processing's legal basis was not indicated.

[39] Council of the European Union, Interinstituional File 2012/0011 (COD), document no. 9788/15, p. 113.

The obligation to indicate a legal basis serves the purpose of allowing the data subject to carry out an examination, albeit a rapid one, as to whether the data processing is presumed to be lawful. In this respect, there is a close connection between legal basis and the obligation to indicate the purposes of the processing. Recital 60 identifies the information as necessary to ensure fair and transparent processing.

The possibility for the controller to invoke previously unmentioned legal bases may lead to a processing which is not foreseeable for the data subject and thus possibly not fair. Sometimes the controller must explain the relevant legal grounds to the data subject on a case-by-case basis and the subsumption of the facts under the relevant legal foundations in full (for such an interpretation, see Bäcker, 2018, Art. 13 mn. 25).

However, the controller is by no means required to enable the data subject to execute a complete legal examination. The indication of the legal basis is purely supplementary. Even within the framework of the access right (Art. 15 GDPR), the legal basis does not have to be indicated, although according to recital 63 this right explicitly pursues the objective of enabling the data subject to verify the processing's lawfulness. If it is not necessary to mention the legal basis even in the context of access, the legislator apparently assumed that the review of legality is the data subject's task. While the controller must establish that the processing can be validly founded on a legal basis, there is no duty to provide the data subject with a thorough legal analysis.

Furthermore, the directory of the processing operations, which must be maintained by the controller, does not foresee a duty to the documentation of the respective legal basis, although this instrument is expressly designed to document the controller's adherence to the GDPR (recital 82). Although a data protection impact assessment serves to ensure the protection of personal data and prove compliance with the provisions of the GDPR (recital 90), even with particularly risky data processing procedures involving a data protection impact assessment according to Art. 35 GDPR, the law does not provide for an obligation to state legal bases (Art. 35 Para. 7 GDPR).

Finally, despite the requirement to take "appropriate measures" to transmit information and protect the fundamental rights of the data subjects under the Charter, it does not seem necessary to provide for such a far-reaching legal consequence and deny the controller the right to rely on possibly unmentioned legal bases.

It is in the controller's interest to be clear about the processing's legal basis not to leave it to chance whether the processing is lawful. If, however, the indication of the legal basis were of central importance for the lawfulness of the processing, an explicit statutory regulation to that effect would have been framed.

The assumption of self-commitment concerning the legal bases mentioned in the information would therefore go far beyond the wording; hence, it must be rejected.

The same question discussed with reference to the legal basis arises about the purposes to be stated by the controller: Should the controller be able to rely on additional purposes, namely to purposes that the controller did not originally refer to, or should this only be prohibited?

In this respect, neither the wording of Art. 13 nor that of Art. 14 GDPR expressly orders such a legal consequence. The possibility of a change of purpose is expressly provided for in Art. 13 para. 3 and Art. 14 para. 4 GDPR. However, the regulation is limited to the fact that the controller must make the information available to the data subject also with regard to the changed purposes following paragraph 2 of Art. 13 or Art. 14 GDPR.

However, from this regulation, it follows in the reverse conclusion that the subsequent adding of purposes must be possible even if such were not mentioned in the original information. Otherwise, Art. 13 (3) and Art. 14 (4) GDPR would have no application scope. In addition, it must be taken into account that Art. 13 and Art. 14 GDPR do not establish any specifications for the admissibility of the change of purpose, which are rather to be found in Art. 6 (4) GDPR, concerning the permissibility of the processing. The questions of information and admissibility are thus regulated in different law places.

The DPD also provided for the possibility of a purpose change. Recital 28 and Art. 6 (1) (b) of the DPD stipulate that the purposes must be clear and legitimate and defined when the data are collected. Further processing after the collection should not be incompatible with the original purpose. However, Articles 10 and 11 of the DPD provided for an obligation to provide information on the purpose of the processing, thus likewise differentiating between information duties and admissibility regulations, and it is not obvious that the legislator in principle wanted to deviate from this concept with the introduction of the GDPR.

In the context of teleological interpretation, too, the question arises as to whether a self-commitment is necessary with a view to the goals of the GDPR concerning the originally designated purposes. A difference exists between the determination of the required purposes according to Art. 5 (1) (b) GDPR and the mere communication of this determination in the context of the information. It is quite conceivable that a controller may define a processing purpose while not specifying it within the information's scope, such as accidentally.

However, the principle of purpose limitation differs in one essential aspect from the previously discussed designation of the legal basis. While the applicability of a legal basis can be objectively determined and legally assessed, the purpose is constitutive for the subsequent legal examination of the processing's lawfulness. Neither the controller nor the data subject may deviate from the objectively applicable law without authorisation. However, the intended purpose is the factual basis to carry out a legal examination of a processing operation's admissibility.

Furthermore, there is an explicit legal link between the communicated purposes and the legal admissibility of a later change of purpose. In accordance with Art. 6 (4) (b), when assessing the admissibility of a change of purpose, the context in which the personal data were originally collected must be taken into account, in particular with regard to the relationship between the data subjects and the controller. According to recital 50, a particular account should be taken of the data subjects' reasonable expectations based on their relationship with the controller. It is evident that reasonable expectations will be primarily based on the information provided by the controller.

In this respect, one may not have to see a change of purpose in every formal deviation of the processing purpose from the previously provided information. However, information decisively deviating from a later processing purpose can be considered a change of purpose, which can then possibly prove incompatible with the original purposes in the weighing of interest prescribed by Art. 6 (4) GDPR.

In this overall assessment, a possible discrepancy between information and processing purpose should not be overestimated since such information is usually not of interest for the vast majority of data subjects, as shown in Chapters 4 and 5. If it is assumed that only about 1% of those concerned are willing to call up data protection information at all (at least in the specific processing context of a website), the other criteria mentioned in Art. 6 para. 4 GDPR (connections between the purposes for which the personal data were collected and those of the intended further processing, the nature of the personal data, the possible consequences of the intended further processing for the data subjects, and the existence of suitable guarantees, which can include encryption or pseudonymisation) are of significantly greater importance.

The information on processing's purposes will have a specific binding effect on the controller if a future purpose is incompatible with the originally communicated purposes in extreme deviation cases. A too restrictive consideration of the information in the context of the compatibility test of the Art. 6 (4) GDPR would, however, overestimate the actual meaning of such information for data subjects.

According to Art. 13 (1) (e) and 14 (1) (e) GDPR, the controller is to provide information about "the recipients or categories of recipients of the personal data, if any". The question arises whether the controller is eligible to choose between disclosing the actual recipients, only categories of recipients (see Paal, 2018, Art. 13 mn. 18, and Franck, 2018, Art. 13 mn. 17), or all recipients, except when they are not able to do that (see Bäcker, 2020, Art. 13 GDPR mn. 30).

Based on the wording, the controller seems to have a free choice, given that the two alternatives are linked by the word "or". While the alternative "recipients" is mentioned before the alternative "categories of recipients", there is no actual order between the two alternatives.

A comparison with other provisions shows that in other circumstances, the legislator expressly restricted the controller's choice as to what kind of information was to be provided. For example, in Art. 13 (2) (a) GDPR, the controller is to provide "the period for which the personal data will be stored, or if that is not possible, the criteria used to determine that period". In this case, the GDPR expressly foresees that in principle, the particular period must be provided, whereas the mere criteria (or "categories") will only suffice if the provision of particular periods "is not possible".

The fact that in Art. 13/13 (1) (e) GDPR no such "possibility" test is prescribed clearly speaks in favour of a free choice of the controller of which information they want to provide.

Already in Art. 10 (c) of the DPD, it was foreseen that the "recipients or categories of recipients" should be subject to an information obligation. However, the DPD did not hint whether the choice between the two alternatives was up to the controller.

The purpose of this information is, again, transparency. However, the meaning of the information must not be overestimated. First, it is important to stress that, as indicated before, few people will actually take notice of the information. As the Article 29 Working Party pointed out, "[i]n accordance with the principle of fairness, controllers must provide information on the recipients that is most meaningful for data subjects. In practice, this will generally be the named recipients, so that data subjects know exactly who has their personal data".[40] However, even this article pointed out that the controller may "opt" to

---

[40] Article 29 Data Protection Working Party, WP 260 (2016), p. 47.

provide only information on the categories of recipients. Moreover, it is not necessarily more meaningful to provide recipients' actual names, as their names may or may not offer any insight as to what kind of recipient they are. While a name such as "Google" may certainly be meaningful to the recipient, lesser-known entities may leave the data subject without any meaningful information as to the processing' criticality. To this end, the provision of categories of recipients (with a meaningful category name such as "marketing agency" or "letter shop") may actually prove to contain more valuable information for the data subject.

Furthermore, the data subject has at all times the right to obtain access per Art. 15 GDPR, whereby they may request information on the recipients or categories of recipients. However, in this context, it is much more arguable that the choice rests with the data subject, as recital 60 (which only speaks of recipients rather than categories of recipients) underpins.

Based on this interpretation of the law, the choice of whether to provide the actual names of recipients or categories of recipients shall principally rest with the controller. Only in extreme cases an argument could be made for a duty to disclose the actual recipients as part of the information, particularly where a mere category would be meaningless for the data subject, and the name of the actual recipient is very meaningful. Those will, however, be rare cases in practice.

A similar question arises concerning the duty to disclose the storage period. According to Art. 13/14 (2) (a) GDPR, "the period for which the personal data will be stored, or if that is not possible, the criteria used to determine that period" must be disclosed. In a recent decision, the European Court of Justice left the question of whether the controller has a choice between disclosing the actual storage periods and disclosing only the criteria for their determination open.[41]

The provision's wording already provides a strong argument against the controller's choice. The provision of the storage periods is mandatory. Only if this is not "possible", the criteria used to determine the period is sufficient.

However, the discussion shifts to the question of what "possible" means in this context. The word "possible" grammatically implies a binary situation: Something is either possible or impossible.[42] To the extent the storage period is known, it will also be possible to indicate it in the data protection information.

---

[41] See ECJ, decision of 01.10.2019, docket no. C-673/17 (Planet49), mn. 79.

[42] See Article 29 Data Protection Working Party, WP 260 (2016), p. 29.

Systematically, Art. 13/14 (2) (a) is crafted as a rule-exception-mechanism: The storage periods must be provided unless this is not possible, in which case an indication of the criteria is sufficient. Hence, as a general rule, the particular storage period must be indicated, and only in exceptional cases will the criteria suffice.

The indication of a storage period is a rather new concept under the GDPR, as it was not included in the DPD. In the original draft of the GDPR, there was no express provision made for an exception: Art. 14 (1) (c) provided that the storage period was to be part of the information.

The recommendations of the European Parliament's Committee on Legal Affairs[43] proposed to generally change the information duty to the information on the criteria for the determination of the storage period. The reason for this was that "[i]t is not always possible to determine exactly for how long personal data is stored, especially in the case of storage for various purposes". [44] This resulted in the compromise that can be found in the GDPR version that was finally passed.

The legislative history thus shows that while the legislator deliberated to allow the controller only to disclose criteria for the storage periods, they clearly decided not to adopt this concept. Only in cases where it is not possible to determine the exact storage period will it suffice to provide criteria.

While the wording, systematic interpretation, and legislative history seem to present a coherent framework, storage periods are actually to be calculated according to the GDPR. While it is possible, in most cases, to give the exact period, this might in practice turn out to be rather the exception than the rule.

The processing of data is permissible as long as the controller can rely on one of the justifications listed in Art. 6 (1) GDPR.[45] Since those justifications can apply simultaneously, the storage period will accordingly last until the very final justification has ceased. For example, a webshop operator may process personal data for the performance of the sale of some good (Art. 6 (1) (b) GDPR). At the same time, they will elect to use personal data for direct marketing purposes (Art. 6 (1) (f) GDPR in connection with recital 47 GDPR). Moreover, under the local tax laws, the controller is legally required (Art. 6 (1)

[43] Recommendations of the European Parliament's Committee on Legal Affairs of 18.10.2012 (2012/0011(COD)), p. 30 f.

[44] Recommendations of the European Parliament's Committee on Legal Affairs of 18.10.2012 (2012/0011(COD)), p. 31.

[45] As long as the processing does not relate to special catergories of personal data, in which case Art. 9 GDPR applies.

(c) GDPR) to keep records of the sale for a certain period of time, such as 10 years. Perhaps, the customer also consented (Art. 6 (1) (a) GDPR) to the receipt of an email newsletter. In other words, it is quite common that several purposes, and their respective storage periods associated with the purpose, will overlap. There may be more than one sales transaction in a continuous customer relationship, resulting in layered storage periods for one and the same purpose (e.g., the storage period for tax purposes will depend on the fiscal year in which the transaction took place).

In such situations, it will be challenging for the controller to precisely calculate the respective storage period for each case. Furthermore, in many cases, the storage period will depend on future developments which are uncertain at the point in time when the information is being collected for the first time (which is generally the point in time in which the information needs to be provided, at least when the data is being collected directly from the data subject). In such cases, it will be a futile attempt to give a precise period, and it will perhaps even lead to misleading or plainly wrong information.

Moreover, in mass processing cases (e.g., the webshop operator has 100,000 customers), it will be impossible for the controller to design data protection information while taking into account the situation a specific individual's situation. Data protection information documents are usually written to provide information for standardized cases, and it will be a commercially impossible attempt to provide each individual with their own customized version of the data protection information.

Considering the underwhelming response data subjects usually show when confronted with data protection information, as lined out in Chapters 4 and 5, it seems inappropriate to apply a too strict approach when determining what is to be considered "possible" within the meaning of Art. 13/14 (2) (a) GDPR.

For practical purposes, despite the seemingly clear wording, systematic analysis and legislative history, it must be taken into account that in many cases the provision of exact storage periods will be, if not physically impossible, a futile and commercially unwarranted attempt. This calls for a lenient and not too strict application of the "possibility" test, which in many cases will allow the controller to provide the criteria for the determination of the storage periods.

6.6 Person Obliged to Provide the Information

In addition to how information must be structured in terms of content and form to meet law requirements, the question arises as to who has to fulfil the information obligations. This question can be subdivided into the questions of who the obligated party is to the standard, namely who has the obligation to secure the information, and whether they have to do this themseves or use third parties. Finally, the question arises as to who is the obligated party in constellations in which more than one person is to be regarded as responsible within the meaning of the GDPR (joint controllership, Art. 26 GDPR).

The wording of Art. 12 (1) sentence 1 GDPR provides a first indication: Accordingly, the controller must take appropriate measures to provide the data subject with the information in accordance with Art. 13 and 13 GDPR. This is confirmed by the specific wording of Art. 13 (1) and (2) and Art. 14 (1) and (2) GDPR, according to which the controller must communicate or make available certain information to the data subject.

In addition to the controller, the processor could be considered apart from the question of who is responsible for fulfilling the information duties in a joint control, which is still to be dealt with separately. However, Art. 28 GDPR, which describes the processor's role and obligations in more detail, does not contain any explicit provisions that would ascribe a legal duty of information to the processor. Art. 30 GDPR also obliges the processor to keep a register of processing activities that must contain all information subject to an information obligation under Art. 13 and 14 GDPR. However, Art. 30 (4) GDPR only stipulates that this list must be made available to the supervisory authority upon request. Art. 30 GDPR does not contain an obligation to make the content available to a data subject, as provided for in Art. 13 and 14 GDPR.

The duties of the data protection officer according to Art. 39 GDPR also do not include the fulfilment of information duties. After analysing the wording, it is evident that the controller should be legally responsible for compliance with the information obligations.

The system of the GDPR's liability regime corresponds to this finding. Pursuant to Art. 82 para. 1 GDPR, liability lies with the controller or processor. However, the latter shall only be liable pursuant to Art. 82 para. 2 sentence 2 GDPR if they have failed to fulfil their obligations under the GDPR specifically imposed on processors or acted in breach of or against the instructions lawfully given by the data controller. Insofar as, contrary to the previous findings, the fulfilment of information obligations does not, for any other reason, constitute an obligation on the part of the processor, the controller is liable for any damage arising from the breach of information obligations. Such reasons cannot be discerned from a systematic point of view either. Rather, Art. 28 para. 3 sentence 2 lit. (e) merely mentions the fact that the processor must assist the data controller in fulfilling their obligation to respond to requests for the exercise of the rights of the data subject set out in Chapter III. Although information obligations are among the "rights of the data subject" in Chapter III, they do not depend on a “request” from the data subject. Nonetheless, it can be inferred from the global reference to Chapter III that the GDPR considers the fulfilment of these obligations as the responsibility of the controller, given that Article 28 (3) sentence 2 (e) GDPR speaks of mere “support” by the processor. The role of the processor in fulfilling all the rights of the data subject should therefore be limited to that of a facilitator. Moreover, even this support duty does not apply ex lege; rather, Art. 28 (3) sentence 2 GDPR stipulates that a contract (or other legal instrument) to be concluded between the responsible party and the processor must provide for such an obligation of support. As a result, it can be deduced from a systematic analysis of the GDPR that the legal obligation to provide information following Articles 13 and 14 applies to the controller.

This interpretation is in line with the legislative history. In its Articles 10 and 11, the DPD already explicitly stipulated that the member states were to provide for the data subject to receive certain information “from the controller or his representative”. It is not apparent that the legislator of the GDPR wanted to deviate from this fundamental concept, since the basic definitions and role descriptions, particularly regarding the role of controllers, have not been significantly changed within the framework of the GDPR.

The apparent purpose of the law also underlines this finding. The information obligations should apply to those who are actually in a position to fulfil them, which requires knowing why and how personal data are processed. However, this corresponds precisely to the legal definition of the data controller, because according to Art. 4 No. 7 GDPR this is the natural or legal person, authority, institution, or other body that alone or jointly with others decides on the purposes and means of the processing of personal data. This is particularly vivid in the German language version of the GDPR. While the English term controller focuses on the aspect of control sovereignty, the German term *Verantwortlicher* addresses their legal responsibility and accountability.

It can therefore be stated that the obligation to provide the information under Articles 13 and 14 GDPR clearly falls on the controller and (apart from the constellation of joint controllers, which is dealt with separately) no other person.

The question also arises as to who should provide the information, namely whether this should be done by the controller themself or can be delegated to third parties.

While Art. 13 and 14 GDPR explicitly mention an act of the controller, Art. 12 (1) sentence 1 GDPR formulates it more generally: According to this provision, the controller only has to take "appropriate measures" to provide the data subject with the necessary information. The wording does not exclude that such measures could also consist in having the necessary information transmitted to the data subject, such as through an intermediary.

There are indications in other provisions of the GDPR that who actually fulfils the duty to provide information is not important. Pursuant to Art. 13 (4) and Art. 14 (5) (a) GDPR, the information obligations do not apply if the data subject already possesses the information. To this end, it cannot make any difference by whom the data subject receives the information because the data controller could avoid their duty to provide it by causing the data subject to receive it by whatever means.

In this respect, too, reference can be made to the predecessor provisions of Art. 10 (1) and Art. 11 (1) of the DPD. However, the DPD explicitly provides for the possibility of the controller transmitting the information through a "representative". This provision is no longer explicitly mentioned in the GDPR, which could lead to assume that it is no longer permissible.

However, whether this divergent wording should be attributed to a substantive change in the law is questionable. The concept of *representative* was not generally defined in the DPD, thus having to be interpreted in the context of the relevant provision. In this respect, the representative's appointment made it clear that the controller did not necessarily have to provide the information in personam. In the GDPR, however, the concept fulfils an entirely different function, a "representative" being "a natural or legal person established in the Union who has been appointed in writing by the controller or processor in accordance with Article 27 and represents the controller or processor in relation to the obligations incumbent upon them under this Regulation". Nonetheless, Art. 27 GDPR stipulates the appointment of a representative established in the EU for controllers who are not established in the EU. The completely changed meaning of the representative would have made it seem inappropriate in the context of information obligations (which apply to controllers within the EU who do not have to appoint an intra-community representative within the meaning of Art. 27 GDPR) to allow fulfilment by a representative. Rather, this would have raised the question of why it is precisely in the context of fulfilling information obligations that the possibility of representation must be expressly addressed, as, although the GDPR addresses many constellations in which representation or assistance by a third party is not only conceivable but can be expected in reality, there is no other reference in it to the possibility of representation, Art. 29 GDPR expressly stipulates that any person subordinate to a controller or a processor may process data on the instructions of the controller. Especially if – as is the rule in business life – the controller for data processing is a legal person, it is unavoidable that they perform their tasks through third parties (corporate bodies or employees) because the legal person as such would otherwise not be able to act. Art. 28 (3) sentence 2 (b) GDPR also expressly recognises that the processor will use certain persons for data processing, who in turn must have undertaken to maintain confidentiality.

If one were to understand the law's silence on the possibility of the de facto fulfilment of the information duties by third parties as the legal exclusion of such a possibility, this would almost thwart the fulfilment of the duties in many constellations.

In addition, it could also be argued within the framework of the DPD – namely, when Art. 10 (1) and Art. 11 (1) of the DPD refer to the fact that the member states only have to provide for information obligations under the condition that the data subject "does not yet have the information in question" – that it did not matter by whom information was actually provided. In this respect, the amended wording cannot be of decisive importance, but the systematic context also suggests that the information does not necessarily have to be personally provided by the controller.

This view can be confirmed when looking at the purpose of the provision. From the interaction between the transparency requirements of Art. 12 GDPR and the specific standards of Art. 13 and 14 GDPR, it becomes clear that, from the point of view of the law, the only decisive factor is to inform the data subject adequately. The value of such information lies in its transparency, namely its ability to inform the data subject of the existence of the processing operation and its purposes. recital 60 GDPR clarifies that the information's main objective is to ensure fair and transparent processing. According to Art. 5 (1) (a) GDPR, the principle of fairness in turn implies the traceability of a processing operation for the data subject. The duty to provide information thus solely focuses on the data subject, whereas the aim of the law is to provide it. As far as the information satisfies the formal quantitative and qualitative requirements in terms of content, from the point of view of the data subject, there is no apparent reason why it should also depend on who, they receive it from.

As a result, it does not matter by whom the necessary information is actually provided. The controller may be represented in the provision of the information or use other means, as long as the relevant data subject is provided with the necessary information.

While the previous discussions were based only on a single controller's basic constellation, the question arises as to whether the result found so far needs to be assessed differently when not one but two or more controllers determine the means and purposes of processing at the same time.

The question plays a significant role in the context of networked systems. For example, websites often incorporate third-party content – so-called plug-ins – which automatically cause specific personal data of the website visitor to be transferred to the provider of the plug-in. According to the European Court of Justice's case-law[46] concerning the collection and transmission of data, both the website and the plug-in providers are to be regarded as jointly responsible within the meaning of Art. 26 GDPR.

Art. 12 to 14 GDPR merely stipulate that "the controller" must provide the information; the law therefore assumes the situation of a single controller.

However, Art. 26 (1) sentence 2 GDPR contains specific provisions on how two or more controllers must comply with the information obligations: The joint controllers determine in an agreement which of them fulfils which obligations under the GDPR concerning the exercise of the data subjects' rights and which of them fulfils which information obligations.[47] In any event, this should apply to the extent that the allocation of tasks is not already regulated by a specific legal provision.

Based on the wording, there are only indirect indications as to who is responsible for the legal obligation to fulfil the information duties in the case of several controllers because the scheme merely requires those responsible to conclude an agreement to that effect. Accordingly, a distinction should be drawn between the situation in which the responsible parties have concluded an agreement to that effect, from which a certain assignment of tasks results in the fulfilment of the information obligations, and the situation in which the responsible parties, contrary to the mandate of Art. 26 (1) sentence 2 GDPR, have not entered into a respective agreement.

In the first constellation, the wording suggests that the legal obligation to fulfil information obligations arises from the agreement reached between the joint controllers. In the second constellation, the wording leaves the result open:

---

[46] See ECJ, judgment of 29.07.2019, case no. C-40/17 (Fashion ID).

[47] As pointed out by the *Amtsgericht* (disctrict court) Mannheim, this could also be the case where the parties believed they were entering into a controller-processor relationship pursuant to Art. 28 GDPR; see AG Mannheim, decision of 11.09.2019, docket no. 5 C 1733/19 WEG, mn. 26.

In the absence of an agreement, there would be no clear assignment of tasks, which could have the consequence that both controllers would be jointly and severally responsible for providing the information. Nonetheless, it is theoretically conceivable that none of those responsible would be subject to such an obligation in the absence of an agreement.

The wording interpretation is also ambiguous because there appear to be relevant differences between the language versions of the GDPR: In the English language version, the agreement is to refer to "their respective duties to provide the information" and thus to the legal obligation, wheres in the German language version, for example, there is talk of "who fulfils which information duties". The German term is linguistically much more closely linked to actual fulfilment than to the legal obligation, which could in turn speak in favour of a purely administrative agreement within the internal relationship.

It follows from recital 79 of the GDPR that a clear allocation of responsibilities serves to protect the rights and freedoms of the data subjects and with regard to the responsibility and liability of those responsible, including measures taken by the supervisory authorities. This justification may suggest an understanding according to which an actual agreement – referred to above as constellation 1 – can in any case have a constitutive effect on the obligations incumbent on a controller. Specifically, if this agreement did not have such a constitutive effect, how the clear allocation of responsibilities laid down in it could have protective effects favouring the data subject or facilitating legal proceedings for the supervisory authorities would not be quite understandable. If such an agreement only has effects in the internal relationship of responsibilities, the data subjects, as well as public authorities, could address both controllers – such as in the event of non-compliance with information obligations – without this entailing any impairment of rights.

However, those provisions of the GDPR which make statements about the legal consequences of a shared responsibility must also be taken into account. Pursuant to Art. 82 (2) GDPR, each controller involved in a processing operation is liable for damage caused by a processing operation that does not comply with the GDPR. According to Art. 82 (3) GDPR, a controller is only released from this liability insofar as they can prove that they are in no way responsible for the circumstances through which the damage occurred. Following Art. 82 (4) GDPR, if more than one controller is involved in the same processing and both are responsible for the damage according to the above provisions, each controller shall be liable for the entire damage to ensure effective compensation for the data subject. At first glance, these provisions seem to contradict the result found on the basis of recital 79 GDPR, as the law in Art. 82 (2) to (4) GDPR in principle assumes joint and several liability of the parties involved and leaves the clarification of different contributions to causation to the internal relationship of those responsible, as the provision in Art. 82 (5) GDPR shows.

However, joint and several liability pursuant to Art. 82 (3) GDPR presupposes that a controller is "responsible for the circumstance through which the damage occurred". Even if the burden of proof for this lies with the controller who wishes to invoke it, liability presupposes that there is a responsibility for a circumstance. However, Art. 82 (3) GDPR does not clarify what a controller is responsible for. If a controller were always jointly responsible for all circumstances of the processing operation, the regulation would have no scope of application. A meaningful application of Art. 82 (3) GDPR rather presupposes that there may be circumstances with several controllers for which one controller is responsible and another not. With this understanding, Art. 82 (2) to (4) GDPR would not preclude the assumption of a legally constitutive character of the agreement concluded pursuant to Art. 26 GDPR.

It is also questionable to what extent the provision in Art. 26 (3) GDPR, according to which the data subject "irrespective of the details of the agreement" may "assert his rights under this Regulation to and against each of the controllers", is applicable.

The first question to be discussed is whether the information obligations fall under the "rights" of the data subject. A *right* is – at least in a bilateral relationship – a claim to demand something from another person who is confronted with a corresponding obligation.

Articles 13 and 14 do not speak of a "right" of the data subject but, conversely, of the controller's obligation. Due to the link between right and duty, however, this may not yet be a decisive argument because if a controller is obliged to act towards the data subject to provide information, the data subject allegedly is, conversely, entitled to such an act.

Art. 26 para. 1 sentence 2 GDPR explicitly differentiates between regulations "concerning the exercise of the rights of the data subject" and regulations on "who fulfils which information duties". According to this wording, the information obligations do not appear to fall under "rights" because otherwise, apart from the reference to "rights" in Chapter III, no separate mention of the information obligations would have been necessary.

The provision in Art. 12 (2) GDPR also gives cause for thought: Suddenly there is only talk of the controller for the data subject "facilitating the exercise of his rights under Articles 15 to 22". Either the legislator saw no reason to encourage the controller to facilitate the exercise of "requests" for the provision of information within the meaning of the previous paragraph, or they assumed that Articles 13 and 14 GDPR, despite their position in Chapter III, did not actually fall under the "rights" of the data subject.

It is also worth noting that Art. 15 of the GDPR expressly states a right to access. If the duty to provide information in this sense were already to be understood as a "right" of the data subject, which conveys a corresponding right to the provision of information, it would be questionable why an explicit right to access was created on top of it. This would be particularly noteworthy, as the duty to provide information and the right to access differ in content: For example, the right of access does not include the legitimate interests, nor the legal basis of the processing, nor the obligation to provide information or the representative's contact details within the EU, all of which are nevertheless part of the information duties under Art. 13/14. Even if one considers the necessity of a separate provision on access because the information under the right to access goes beyond the (proactive) duty to provide information – for example concerning the right to receive a copy of a data – the access right would at least cover the entire scope of the information duties under Art. 13/14.

This speaks against accepting a corresponding claim and thus a "right" of the data subject to the information mentioned in Art. 13/14 GDPR and in favour of a purely one-sided obligation of the controller, the violation of which may lead to sanctions, but – in contrast to the access according to Art. 15 GDPR – does not establish a "right" of the data subject. However, there are doubts as to whether this phenomenon cannot be rather attributed to editorial inaccuracy. Nonetheless, the fact that Art. 13 and Art. 14 are located in Chapter III of the GDPR, which is explicitly entitled "Rights of the data subject", provides an argument for classifying the information duties as a counterpart to a "right" of the data subject.

In addition, the law seems to assume in various places that information pursuant to Art. 13 or 14 GDPR can also be "requested" by the data subject. The first sentence of Article 12(1) of the GDPR states, first, that the controller must provide the "information referred to in Articles 13 and 13 and any communication under Articles 15 to 22" in a particular form. The term "information" is being used only in relation to Articles 13 and 14, while information in relation to Articles 15 et seq. is referred to as "communications". In sentence 3, the concept of *information* (and not "communication") is taken up to the effect that, "if requested by the data subject", the information may also be provided orally in certain circumstances. This thus expresses that there may be a "request" from the data subject for the provision of "information" within the meaning of Articles 13 and 14 GDPR. This is in line with the provision chosen in Art. 12 (5), in which the legislator explicitly saw a need to regulate manifestly unfounded or excessive "applications", including information pursuant to Articles 13 and 14 GDPR (sentence 1).

In this respect, no convincing systematic arguments can be put forward against an understanding of information as the "right" of the data subject.

The DPD already knew of the responsible party's information duties, which were, however, explicitly referred to as "information rights" at that time. Recital 42 of the DPD states that the member states may, under certain circumstances, "restrict the data subject's rights of access and information". The striking feature of this wording is the distinction between rights of access and rights to information, which clarifies that the data subject's rights to information in the DPD can apparently come alongside the right of access.

Although the explicit designation as "right to information" was not continued in the GDPR, there is no reason to consider this as a rejection by the legislator of the "right to information" (in the sense of a claim by the data subject). Rather, the dichotomy of information and access reveals a continuation in the classification of information right as an independent legal institution alongside the concept of access.

The purpose of the information would make it very questionable why the controller should be obliged to provide information, but the data subject should not be allowed to request it. On the one hand, there is no recognisable interest worthy of protection on the controller's part in withholding such information from the data subject. On the other hand, Art. 13 and 14 GDPR precisely serve the interests of the data subject. In view of the right of the data subject to an "effective remedy" (Art. 79 (1) GDPR), it would appear contradictory to consider Art. 13 and 14 GDPR merely as an obligation, the violation of which should be sanctionable by the supervisory authorities but not enforceable by the data subject.48 Such an understanding would possibly also contradict the principle of transparency (Art. 5 para. 1 lit. a) GDPR), according to which personal data may only be processed "in a manner comprehensible to the data subject".

In this respect, there is much to be said in favour of classifying the information obligations of Articles 13 and 14 GDPR as the "rights" of the data subject. Accordingly, the information duty would fall under the term "rights under this Regulation" within the meaning of Art. 26 (3) GDPR.

---

[48] See also *Arbeitsgericht* (labour Court) Düsseldorf (Germany), decision of 05.03.2020, docket no. 9 Ca 6557/18, mn. 55, that seems to treat Art. 13 GDPR as a possible cause of action for the data subject.

It is, however, still questionable what is meant by the power of the data subject to "exercise" their rights under the GDPR "in respect of and against" each of the controllers (Art. 26 para. 3 GDPR), irrespective of what the agreement between the controllers may say. It is questionable whether the rule means that, although the data subject may submit their application to any of the controllers in the sense of a "single point of contact", the information claim is only enforceable against the controller who, in accordance with the agreement, is responsible for fulfilling the information obligations, or whether the data subject may enforce its right to information against the controller of their choice.

The wording is not entirely clear. On the one hand, it is noticeable that the law speaks of "exercise". The term exercise refers to substantive enforcement. By contrast, the term geltend Machen used in the German language version could also be interpreted as a "single point of contact". The Spanish language version (ejercer los derechos), the French language version (exercer les droits), and the Italian language version (esercitare i propri diritti) also seem to speak in favour of an actual enforceability of rights.

It can also be observed that the language versions of the GDPR are not coherent. For example, the term *geltend machen* in the German language version is translated into English as "exercise" within Art. 26 (3) GDPR. However, in Art. 18 (1) (c) GDPR, the term *Geltendmachung* corresponds to the English term "establishment", while the German term *Ausübung*, which much more closely resembles a legal enforcement, is translated as "exercise". Hence not too much emphasis should be put on the actual wording, since the various language versions show that the words have not always been selected with the greatest of care.

No particular inference can be drawn based on the legislative history on the question of how the term *exercise* is to be interpreted within the meaning of Art. 26 (3) GDPR. The original draft did not contain any particular provisions on how the agreement between the controllers might influence the way data subjects may exercise their rights.

The purpose of the provision seems to be aimed at easing the exercising of rights for the data subject. Irrespective of what the joint controllers agree, the data subject should be able to exercise their rights.

This aim can be best achieved if the meaning of Art. 26 (3) GDPR is not limited to a purely administrative one. It would be of little use for the data subject if, even though they can approach each joint controller about an information right, the enforcement of such approach would be subject to the joint controllers' agreement. To this end, it is advantageous to allow the data subject to enforce its rights (including the right to obtain the information according to Art. 13/14 GDPR) against any of the joint controllers, irrespective of their internal agreement.

Art. 26 (3) GDPR should therefore be understood so that the data subject may demand the provision of information according to Art. 13/14 GDPR from any of the joint controllers, irrespective of their internal agreement.

Although not absolutely conclusive, a systematic analysis reveals that in case of joint controllership, the law most likely assumes that each joint controller is responsible for providing the information according to Art. 13/14 GDPR.

The DPD did not contain any regulations on who was responsible for fulfilling information duties – or any data protection obligations at all in the case of joint controllers. The DPD already assumed in the definition of "controller" that a plurality of such controllers could exist. It defined the controller as "the natural or legal person, public authority, agency or any other body which alone or jointly with others decides on the purposes and means of the processing of personal data". However, it did not contain more specific provisions on the consequences of such a constellation.

However, a remarkable development can be observed in the history of the development of the GDPR text. In the Commission's original draft (Art. 24 at the time), the provision contained the following provisions:

"In all cases where a controller determines the purposes, conditions and means of the processing of personal data jointly with other persons, the latter shall jointly agree which of them shall exercise which of their functions under this Regulation, in particular as regards procedures and mechanisms enabling data subjects to exercise their rights".

Compared to the current text of the law, the draft still spoke of "tasks", while the current text of Art. 26 GDPR speaks of "obligations". While the term *task* means the actual implementation and suggests the understanding of a purely administrative internal agreement, the term *obligation* takes up the legally binding character and thus seems to speak for the fact that the agreement reached between the responsible parties should have effects on the obligations affecting the parties involved.

After the publication of the Commission's draft, the report of the Committee on Civil Liberties, Justice and Home Affairs of 16.01.2013 provided for amendment 181, which should have added the following passage to Article 24: "In the absence or ambiguity of such a definition, the data subject may exercise his or her rights vis-à-vis controllers who are jointly and severally liable".

Amendment 181 did not contain any justification. However, the wording of amendment 143 of the opinion of 28.01.2013 of the Committee on the Internal Market and Consumer Protection was taken over by the committee with nearly the same wording, arguing that this provision would give the data subject "greater protection in the specific case". This justification only makes sense if one does not assume that several controllers, irrespective of any existing agreement, never have to jointly guarantee the fulfilment of duties such as information duties.

This regulatory idea was also taken up in further discussions. Regarding Art. 24, a document dated 17.10.2013 outlining a compromise between the European Parliament and the European Council states:

„The arrangement shall duly reflect the joint controllers' respective effective roles and relationships vis-à-vis data subjects, and the essence of the arrangement shall be made available for the data subject. In case of unclarity of the responsibility, the controllers shall be jointly and severally liable".

In this version, the draft was given into parliamentary reading. In a position of the European Parliament adopted at first reading on 12.03.2014, the following addition to the Commission draft was therefore adopted:

"The Agreement shall duly reflect the respective actual functions and relationships of joint controllers vis-à-vis data subjects and the core of the Agreement shall be made available to data subjects. In the event of unclear responsibilities, the controllers shall be jointly and severally liable".

This, too, leads to the understanding that a sufficiently clear definition of responsibilities in an agreement can impact the scope of the legal obligations affecting a controller.

The European Council addressed the issue with a different approach. In a note of the Presidency of the Council of 30.06.2014, a paragraph 2 of Art. 24 was foreseen, which provided for the following:

„Irrespective of the terms of the arrangement referred to in paragraph 1, the data subject may exercise his or her rights under this Regulation in respect of and against each of the (...) controllers unless the data subject has been informed in a transparent manner which of the joint controllers is responsible"

The following explanation can be found in the associated footnote 214:

„DE [and] FR emphasised that it would be in the interest of the data subject to have clear rules which allow it to address its requests to all controllers concerned. Potential language problems in case of controllers established in different Member States were also highlighted. ES indicated that such arrangements can never be to the detriment of the data subject's rights and its proposal for paragraph 2 seeks to take account of the concerns".

Here, for the first time, the idea is found that even a sufficiently clear agreement need not per se lead to a limitation of the obligations of a responsible person, up to the most restrictive view of Spain, according to which an agreement between responsible persons must never be to the detriment of a data subject.

In the official proposal of the European Council Presidency of 11 June 2015, the regulatory proposals were again modified and included in a general orientation declaration. They stated:

„1. … The arrangement shall designate which of the joint controllers shall act as single point of contact for data subjects to exercise their rights.

2. Irrespective of the terms of the arrangement referred to in paragraph 1, the data subject may exercise his or her rights under this Regulation in respect of and against each of the (…) controllers.

3. The arrangement shall duly reflect the joint controllers' respective effective roles and relationships vis-à-vis data subjects, and the essence of the arrangement shall be made available for the data subject. Paragraph 2 does not apply where the data subject has been informed in a transparent and unequivocal manner which of the joint controllers is responsible, unless such arrangement other than one determined by Union or Member State law is unfair with regard to his or her rights (…)".

The proposal was accompanied by the following reservations in the associated footnote 402:

„SI reservation […] warned against potential legal conflicts on the allocation of the liability and […] therefore thought this article should be further revisited in the context of the future debate on Chapter VIII. FR also thought the allocation of liability between the controller and the processor is very vague, and CZ expressed doubts about the enforceability of this provision in the private sector outside arrangements within a group of undertakings and thought it should contain a safeguard against outsourcing of responsibility".

In the reservations, Slovenia addresses possible contradictions to the liability regime. Indeed, it is unclear how the proposal would affect the constellation where an agreement assigns the responsibility for providing information to one of several responsible parties. Nevertheless, due to the more far-reaching condition of disclosure of the essence of the agreement, a data subject could only have relied on the person designated in the agreement to assert their rights under this proposal had the agreement not been considered unfair.

In preparation for the trialogue between the European Commission, the European Council, and the European Parliament, the Committee of Permanent

Representatives of the Member States adapted the regulation in a further compromise text. In Art. 24, the proposed restriction of the data subject's recourse against any of the controllers was omitted. This would have meant that the agreement could not have had any constitutive effect concerning the exercise of rights vis-à-vis the data subject with regard to the scope of the data protection catalogue of obligations.

This suggests, however, that the associated downgrading of the meaning of the content of such an agreement did not appear to have been intended. Rather, this development also speaks for the constitutional character of such an agreement, especially concerning the information obligations explicitly mentioned in Art. 26 GDPR.

Regardless of the legislative history and what the various parties involved in the legislation might have considered, objectively, the phenomenon of joint controllers is a favourable one for the data subject. Instead of only one controller, the data subject may now rely on two or more controllers who in principle are jointly and severally liable towards him.

Leaving it to the controllers to decide who ultimately bears a legal responsibility to provide the information would seem to run counter to this concept. As the analysis of Art. 26 (3) GDPR has shown, the information corresponds to a respective "right" of the data subject. The information is not a merely administrative obligation, and, while Chapters 4 and 5 show that data subjects usually do not pay much attention to the data protection information, there is no compelling reason why they should not be jointly liable for providing the required information.

The interpretation of the law shows superior arguments for each of the joint controllers' legal duty to provide the information required under Art. 13/14.

6.7 Administrative Fines

Finally, the questions arise of what kind of administrative fines the controller will suffer if they fail to comply with the information duties and which role the findings in Chapters 4 and 5 may play in determining the fine.

According to Art. 83 (1) GDPR, administrative fines in each individual case shall "be effective, proportionate and dissuasive". Art. 83 (2) GDPR goes on listing the factors that shall be given "due regard" when determining the fine amount. Those are:

- the nature, gravity, and duration of the infringement, taking into account the nature, scope, or purpose of the processing concerned as well as the number of data subjects affected and the level of damage suffered by them;

- the intentional or negligent character of the infringement;
- any action taken by the controller or processor to mitigate the damage suffered by data subjects;
- the degree of responsibility of the controller or processor, taking into account technical and organisational measures implemented by them pursuant to Articles 25 and 32;
- any relevant previous infringements by the controller or processor;
- the degree of cooperation with the supervisory authority, to remedy the infringement and mitigate its possible adverse effects;
- the categories of personal data affected by the infringement;
- the manner in which the infringement became known to the supervisory authority, in particular, whether the controller or processor notified the infringement, and, if so, to what extent;
- compliance with measures referred to in Article 58 (2) whenever they were previously ordered against the controller or processor concerned with regard to the same subject-matter;
- adherence to approved codes of conduct pursuant to Article 40 or approved certification mechanisms pursuant to Article 42; and
- any other aggravating or mitigating factor applicable to the circumstances of the case, such as financial benefits gained or losses avoided, directly or indirectly, following the infringement.

This work shall now examine each factor and determine its role in light of the results.

One factor is "the nature, gravity and duration of the infringement taking into account the nature scope or purpose of the processing concerned as well as the number of data subjects affected and the level of damage suffered by them". This factor emphasizes the overall assessment of the infringement. According to recital 148 GDPR, in case of a minor infringement or if the fine likely to be imposed would constitute a disproportionate burden to a natural person, a reprimand may be issued instead of a fine. This emphasizes that a fine is not mandatory in all cases. In "minor" cases, other legal consequences come into play.

When considering what kind of infringements are possible under the GDPR, the violation of information duties under Art. 13/14 should not be considered overly serious. The greatest detrimental effect will result from illegal processing and not from the breach of a more or less bureaucratic provision.

As the results in Chapters 4 and 5 show, data protection information is generally viewed by data subjects as not significantly relevant. Furthermore, there cannot be found a general indifference to the provision of certain information, as can be seen with regard to the access numbers on the imprint subpage. Apparently, obtaining such basic information about the provider's identity is much more frequent than acquiring it about data processing, although also on a comparably low level.

Furthermore, the gravity is, inter alia, determined by the "level of damage suffered" by the data subjects. It is hard to imagine data subject suffering any damage from a failure to provide proper information alone. To this end, the infringement upon information duties should generally be considered a minor infringement. It would be not warranted to consider a violation of the data privacy information as a grave infringement. Here is where the above findings in Chapters 4 and 5 must be taken into account. It would be hard to argue that the failure to provide information caused any damage when the data show that, in fact, virtually no one would have acknowledged the information, let alone base a purchase decision on such information. Failure to provide information that virtually nobody ever accesses can hardly be found to be an infringement of great gravity.

Naturally, the intentional or negligent character of the infringement will depend on the specific case's circumstances. Given the many uncertainties around the information duties, however, it seems advisable not to be too fast in accepting an intentional conduct. Many shortcomings around the information duties will be unintentional and simply due to the fact that the law is in many ways formulated in an unclear manner.

The law speaks of mitigating actions taken by the controller regarding "the damage suffered by data subjects". While assessing any mitigating actions will be subject to the individual case, it is hard to imagine what kind of damages the data subject might have suffered solely based on missing, wrongful, or incomplete information.

To this end, mitigating actions may encompass providing the updated necessary information to the data subjects. However, failure to do so should not be considered a relevant factor for determining the number of administrative fines in the context of information duties. As the results in Chapters 4 and 5 show, data subjects rarely take an interest in data protection information. Hence, repeated or updated information will most likely not significantly improve the average data subject's viewpoint.

In a single controller situation, it is hard to imagine how the controller could argue that they only had a diminished degree of responsibility. However, in joint controller constellations, the joint controller agreement can be considered.

While the analysis revealed that the internal agreement between joint controllers will not influence the legal responsibility to provide information under Art. 13/14 GDPR as such, it may still play a role if the task to provide the information is clearly delegated to one of the joint controllers with the other joint controllers relying on that controller's fulfilment of the information duty. In such cases, the degree of responsibility of the other controllers may diminish, whereas a high degree of responsibility should be placed onto the controller who, according to the joint controller agreement, took the task to provide the information.

The factor of relevant previous infringements may only be considered in specific circumstances. A repeated violation of information duties could certainly be an aggravating factor.

The degree of cooperation is also a factor that must be assessed in the individual circumstances. However, such cooperation is not a relevant factor as such but only if it occurs or fails to occur "in order to remedy the infringement and mitigate the possible adverse effects of the infringement". The law anticipates that the infringement brings about adverse effects and possibly even damages which need to be mitigated. Where, however, there are no adverse effects or damages, as will usually be the case when information duties have been infringed, the degree of cooperation with the supervisory authority plays a much lesser role than in cases of actual unlawful data processing.

This factor assumes that personal data have been "affected by the infringement", which makes sense in cases of unlawful processing but seems to be of little use in the case of an infringement of information duties. As a maximum, it seems viable to use this factor only where the information duty related to special categories of personal data.

In the specific circumstances, the manner in which the infringement became known to the supervisory authority – in particular, whether the controller or processor notified the infringement, and, if so, to what extent – plays a role.

This is aimed at punishing a controller who keeps an infringement "in secret" rather than openly communicating it. When it comes to information duties, however, an infringement will rarely be "secret". Due to the nature of the data protection information according to Art. 13/14 GDPR, many infringements will already be plainly visible. This means that at least no aggravating emphasis should be put on a controller who actively fails to notify the supervisory authority of such infringement.

The compliance with previously ordered measures may be a factor, although most likely presumably in very few cases.

The adherence to approved codes of conduct or approved certification mechanisms may play a more prominent role in the future. Currently, there are only very few, if any, approved codes of conduct or certification mechanisms in place.

According to this factor, any other aggravating or mitigating factor applicable to the case's circumstances, such as financial benefits gained or losses avoided, directly or indirectly, following the infringement, may be considered. This opens the assessment of factors not expressly mentioned in Art. 83 (2) GDPR. However, failure to comply with information duties will rarely result in financial benefits or the avoidance of losses. While it may certainly require some effort to draft up a data protection notice, the associated costs will hardly influence the controller's decision. On the contrary, it is worth pointing out that the controller usually wins nothing if they fail to comply with information duties. Since Chapters 4 and 5 showed how seldomly people bother accessing (let alone reading) the information, it seems unlikely that controllers can significantly benefit from omitting such information.

Even if the information on how data is being processed is provided to users and users originally have no intention of disclosing personal information altogether (whether based on a general reluctance or the actual information provided in the privacy policy), it has been demonstrated that such intention is not a reliable indicator of the users' actual behaviour. This finding also invalidates any notion of privacy information being essential to enable self-determination of consumers.

The factors that need to be considered when assessing a fine will depend on the specific circumstances. However, in cases of infringement of information duties for a number of factors, they will rather serve as mitigating factors, leading to a comparatively lower amount of administrative fines. In cases of one-time violations of information duties, in the absence of any aggravating factors in the individual case, it would even be arguable to consider the infringement "minor" and omit an administrative fine altogether (in favour of a reprimand as per recital 148).

The data protection authorities practice seems to confirm this view. Depending on the country in which the fine is imposed, the average ranges between €2,500 and €5,500, with the median being around €2,000. To this end, the data protection authorities seem to appropriately apply the criteria laid down in the GDPR for the assessment of fines.

Pursuant to Art. 83 (4) and (5) GDPR, there a two categories of fines: one with a framework of up to the higher of €10 million or 2% of the annual worldwide turnover, and one with a framework of €20 million or 4% of the annual worldwide turnover. Interestingly, a violation of the information duties belongs to the second category, which threatens the higher fine. The legislator obviously held that an infringement of the information duties must be considered a major one, compared to infringements of the first category, which contains, among others, infringements against the regulations concerning a child's consent (Art. 8 GDPR) and against the obligations of a data processor (Art. 28 GDPR) and even the notification of the individual in cases of a personal data breach (Art. 34 GDPR). In other words, the fine framework for failing to provide general information on how data is being processed is surprisingly higher than for failing to inform a person if that individual's personal data have been accidentally disclosed to third parties, which is likely to result in a high risk to the rights and freedoms of natural persons (Art. 34 (1) GDPR), such as if credit card information has been disseminated into the dark web.

It is important to note that the role of Art. 83 (4) and (5) GDPR is limited to the provision of an upper ceiling of a potential administrative fine. The category to which an infringement belongs is not a factor in determining the actual amount of the fine; otherwise, it would have been relatively easy for the legislator to include it as an express factor in Art. 83 (2) GDPR. This is in line with recital 150 GDPR, which expressly differentiates between the criteria for setting the fines (equivalent to the factors in paragraph 2 of Art. 83 GDPR) and the upper limits (equivalent to paragraphs 4 and 5 of Art. 83 GDPR).

It seems that with the implementation of the GDPR, the lawmakers significantly overestimated the relevance of privacy information, which is surprising, given that the consumer's indifference to privacy information has been established for many years. While this does not seem to make much sense, it is a decision which needs to be accepted, although, given the low importance placed upon privacy information by individuals, as pointed out in Chapters 4 and 5, it seems de lege ferenda worthwhile to revisit this classification in a future update of the GDPR. Hence, when controllers fail to provide the information according to Art. 13 GDPR, the imposition of a severe fine would generally not be warranted, except for the individual case's special circumstances.

If this applies to cases of complete failure to provide the information, it must apply all the more to cases where the information has been provided but merely failed to adhere to the required level of concise, transparent, intelligible, and easily accessible form and clear and plain language (Art. 12 (1) GDPR). This will be the most practically relevant issue because most websites provide some sort of privacy information due to legal requirements or best practice.

As was shown above, the vast majority of users will never be impacted by an insufficiently transparent formulation of privacy information, as they do not access this information in the first place. This should call authorities for a more lenient approach when it comes to the administering of fines.

7 SUMMARY OF FINDINGS

7.1 Summary of Legal Analysis

The present work has established, based on a real-life analysis of access numbers, that at least in an internet context, the ratio between uses accessing (not necessarily reading) a data protection information and the total number of website visitors is remarkably low – on average, around .3% (median: .75%).

This result plays a significant role in the legal interpretation of a number of questions arising in the context of information duties under Art. 13 and 14 GDPR.

7.1.1 Concise and Transparent Form

The "concise and transparent form" requirement in Article 12 GDPR must be treated with caution. Specifically, it should not be interpreted in a sense that completeness in terms of every detail was required. It is sufficient to have a detailed enough text that the data subject can roughly assess the risk associated with the data processing activity.

7.1.2 Language and Accessibility

The information must in principle be provided in the national language of the place where the services associated with the processing are actively offered and directed. The controller should provide information in additional languages only in exceptional circumstances. Usually, where privacy information is offered in text form, this will usually satisfy the "accessibility" test.

7.1.3 Point in Time When the Information Needs to be Provided

Where data are being collected from the data subject, a simultaneous provision of the information is sufficient. When data are not being collected directly from the data subject, Art. 14 GDPR allows a reasonable period of time for information, at the latest within one month. However, if the data are used for communication with the data subject or disclosed to a recipient, the information must only be provided at the latest at the time of the first communication to the data subject or the first disclosure, even if this is much later than the one month period.

When a change of purpose occurs, one-time information in case an additional purpose is sufficient. The information needs not to be repeated every time the data is being processed for the additional purpose. In cases of consent, the information required for a valid consent needs to be present before or at least at the same time when the consent is being declared.

7.1.4 Form of Information

The controller may in principle choose in which form to provide the information. Exceptions exist with regard to the oral provision, which is only permissible if requested by the data subject. This request can also be implied and does not need to be express.

In principle, information may also be provided electronically, except where there are reasonable grounds to believe that the data subject is not using electronic means of communication. Usually, however, internet access can be assumed.

7.1.5 Selected Information Content

While the controller needs to disclose the legal bases and purposes for which they process personal data, such information does not exclude the controller from relying on additional legal bases or purposes even if they were not mentioned in the original data protection information. However, the information on the purposes of processing will have a certain binding effect on the controller if a future purpose proves incompatible with the originally communicated purposes, as in cases of extreme deviation. Still, the original purposes must not be interpreted too restrictively.

With regard to the disclosure of recipients of personal data, the controller may choose whether to provide the actual names of recipients or only categories of recipients, except for extreme cases. With regard to the information on the storage period, there is generally no such choice. However, it must be taken into account that in many cases the provision of exact storage periods will realistically be not possible. Hence, in many cases, the controller should be allowed to only provide the criteria to determine the storage periods.

7.1.6 Person to Provide the Information

The controller is obliged to provide the information under Art. 13 and 14 GDPR. However, it does not matter whether they offer it in person or through an intermediary, as long as they eventually provide the necessary information to the relevant data subject. In a joint controllership scenario, each of the joint controllers is to provide the information required under Art. 13 and 14 GDPR.

7.1.7 Administrative Fines

While the amount of a fine for failure to provide proper information will depend on the specific circumstances, an analysis of the relevant determination factors shows that penalties must be comparatively low, if not even omittable.

Insufficient privacy information will not significantly impact the vast majority of data subjects, which should call administrative authorities for both a lenient approach and a redetermination of the information duties and the fine regime in a future revision of the GDPR.

7.2 Practical Implications for Enterprises

Given the boundaries of this work, the analysis reveals an ambiguous result: On the one hand, the data suggest that information plays a relatively small role from the individual's viewpoint. Given how few users are actually willing to access the data protection information, it is hard to believe that this information could be relevant for the individual's decision on the continued use of the service. The analysis confirms that many people do not cherish their data privacy – a phenomenon that easily explains the marked success of Google, Facebook, and other internet giants.

On the other hand, the legal framework seems to be extremely tight. The GDPR takes a strong focus on transparency and information duties, apparently based on the assumption that providing the necessary information to individuals was crucial for their informed and responsible use of the internet. Unfortunately, people seem to be quite reluctant to make any use of the information.

A number of conclusions can be drawn from the results of this work for practice. First of all, the focus should be on the law user, namely companies and other bodies that process personal data. They are in a quandary: On the one hand, they are exposed to strict obligations, at least on paper, the violation of which can in any case potentially be punished with high fines. On the other hand, the provision of information threatens to degenerate into a formality if one considers that the individuals concerned will not read it for the most part. Nevertheless, it is recommended that companies invest sufficient care in the information because, even if the supervisory authorities' practice has not resulted in the imposition of excessively high fines, a company will not be able to rely on this. Furthermore, there may be an interaction between the information obligations and data processing lawfulness requirements. Since the GDPR requires processing in good faith, processing for purposes not mentioned in the data protection information could be considered in bad faith under certain circumstances. Therefore, companies would do well to reflect the processing purposes pursued in the privacy notice as completely and accurately as possible.

Moreover, investigations by the supervisory authority could extend to other data protection issues with potentially more severe consequences even in an initially comparatively minor breach of information obligations. Hence, it certainly makes sense to offer as little surface for attack as possible from the outset, especially since data protection information – at least if it is on websites – is visible to everyone and thus also to the supervisory authorities. Potential breaches, therefore, have an increased risk of detection.

7.3 Implications for the Future of the Transparency Principle

The research results show that the European legislator massively overestimates the transparency principle. While the principle is definitely an advantage for those who are specifically looking for certain information on data processing, it is an unnecessary advantage for most data subjects. In many cases, the information provided is not used. The strict requirements that are sometimes placed on the content, form, and level of detail of the information seem excessive. If one takes into account the actual use of the information provided, there ultimately is considerable overlap with regard to the right to information (i.e., right to access), which allows every interested party to obtain nearly the same information in terms of content that is already the subject of the information obligations. In this respect, it is not justifiable to burden the controllers with both duties at the same time. Even if no studies exist on this, it can be assumed that in view of the formally high threat of fines, companies make considerable efforts to provide data protection information that is as unassailable as possible. Since I have provided 40 to 50 companies with data protection declarations in the course of my work as a lawyer, I can argue from experience that there is no tangible advantage for either companies or data subjects. It may seem obvious to impose information on the party that is most likely or most favourably able to make the effort required for it (cheapest cost avoider). In reality, however, the question is not which of the two parties should sensibly be burdened with an information obligation but whether such information is necessary at all for the intended transaction, be it the use of a website or the utilisation of a service. As the results of the present work have shown, this is not the case. On the contrary, virtually all users decide for or against the use of a service without regard to the privacy policy's content. If this is the case, then the issue cannot be who should be subject to an information obligation but whether an information obligation is necessary at all. This is to be negated here.

In this respect, the transparency principle would still be sufficiently taken into account by granting the data subject - as provided for in Art. 15 GDPR – a right to information. With the help of this right, every data subject would be able to easily request the information relevant to them from a controller if they considered it relevant for whatever reason. For controllers, this would have the advantage of only having to provide the information to those individuals who actually have an interest in it. Proactive information that is imposed on the data subject without them actually wanting to take note of it does not serve a reasonable purpose.

7.4 "Cookie" Banners

The phenomenon of imposed information can currently be observed vividly in the cookie banners found on websites. After the courts ruled that so-called cookies – small files that serve to identify an end device by the website provider – may in many cases only be used with the active consent of the internet user, websites all over Europe are covered by cookie banners or cookie walls. The user only gets to see the website's actual content after making a more or less discriminating choice between different consent options. Here, too, case law has set stringent standards for the so-called informed consent. This means that if website providers want to use cookies, they are forced to provide the user with extensive information texts to enable an informed decision. However, most users do not want to make such a decision, which is why even today most cookie banners are confirmed by the user. Since politicians have now also recognised that such a flood of information is not in the interest of the user who actually feels hindered by it, voices have already been raised calling for the abolition of cookie consent with comprehensive information texts. In this reflection process, it would be extremely beneficial to take the present study results into account, for it could hardly be more powerfully demonstrated that users are primarily interested in the simplicity and usefulness of the respective offers, whereas information on data protection is mostly understood as a necessary but irrelevant evil.

The situation can be compared to the package inserts of medicines: Most people take a headache tablet without thinking about the medicine's composition and side effects. Only in exceptional cases are these documents studied carefully. However, while it may still be acceptable in the case of the protection of life and health that manufacturers must also provide appropriate documentation (and print a lot of paper for this purpose) to those who will never take note of this information, such an instrument does not seem appropriate in the case of personal data protection. This is all the more true if one considers – as explained above – that with the right of access, an almost equally effective instrument is available with which every data subject can request the relevant information (and even more).

7.5 Proposal for a Revision of the GDPR

In this respect, it is only appropriate to advise the legislator in a future revision of the GDPR to considerably restrict the duty to provide information or even to abolish it altogether. Instead, it would make sense to refer the data subject to the right to information. The threat of a fine in the event of a breach of information obligations – which is high in abstract terms, at any rate – should also be reconsidered. Such punishment seems to be completely excessive – especially in relation to other, sometimes much more serious offences. The question arises as to whether a separate offence of a fine is needed here at all or whether it would not be sufficient to punish the failure to provide information requested by a data subject with a fine.

8 DISCUSSION

8.1 Limits and Boundaries of this Work

Before discussing the results, it is necessary to consider where the present study's limits lie. On the one hand, the data on the retrieval of privacy information were collected in the context of the internet. It is well known that the use of the internet is highly fleeting and often relatively inattentive. Users tend to look for quick and unproblematic access to information. Hence, they are often neither used to nor interested in reading long and legally formulated texts first. Sometimes they will probably also assume that the use should already be "ok", namely not posing any particular risks to their own rights and fundamental freedoms, not least because of the legal framework. This negligence may be partly attributable to the perceived high level of protection that emanates from the GDPR. It would be thus helpful in the future to investigate whether users located in jurisdictions without strong data protection legislation neglect data protection information in the same way. If this were the case, one would probably be able to assume that the actual or perceived level of protection does not play a decisive role in user behaviour.

Similarly, the present study was not able to show to what extent the access figures vary depending on the nature of the website or the typical user group of such a website. It is conceivable, for example, that older, more experienced internet users who are aware of the dangers of data processing show a greater interest in data protection information than young or adolescent users. Likewise, differences may show up depending on users' gender or educational levels. Such differences could not be examined in the present study. Depending on the respective evaluation tools (e.g., Google Analytics), the access figures could, however, be selected according to further socio-demographic criteria, so that, in principle, even more detailed evaluations may be carried out with the methodology used here.

8.2 Alternative Approaches

It might be worth paying greater attention to the approaches set out in Art. 12(7) and (8) GDPR. The law already provides that information can also be conveyed by standardised pictorial symbols. In any case, the studies found in the literature, such as those by Kelley and McDonald, partly suggest that colour or picture symbols are understood by the user significantly better and faster than more or less extensive texts. Unfortunately, the European Commission has not yet made use of its power to adopt a procedure for the provision of standardised picture symbols. However, as can be seen from other areas, symbols and colours that are easy to perceive visually can provide the customer with a basic understanding of specific characteristics of the performance. If, for example, energy efficiency classes can be communicated by means of symbols or traffic light systems, it is hard to see why this could not also be a suitable approach in data protection law. This is at least true if the requirements for information duties – as argued in this paper – are not seen as too strict.

8.3 Criticism against this work's findings

The findings of this work present a dilemma: One the one hand, the work shows that data protection information is often of little practical use and does not significantly affect the behaviour of individuals. But this finding does not solve the problem of how to make data protection work in practice. Particularly in cases where the legitimacy of data processing relies on the action of an individual, as is the case where the data processing is based on the individual's consent, the question is to which degree the assessment of such behaviour should be based on how well the individual was informed about the consequences of their action. The solution could either be to treat the action (e.g. the consent) as legally non-effective if a defined level of information has not been secured, or to neglect the level of information, provided the individual decided to proceed with the action regardless of the lack of information.

Treating the action is legally non-effective is the way preferred by both the majority of authors and the public data protection authorities. This logic shifts the legal risk entirely on the data processing entity, while the individual enjoys a maximum level of protection. It would be compliant with the "data-protection-friendly" approach championed by data protection authorities and the European Court of Justice's jurisprudence. But this approach comes at a cost: For example, an internet user may choose to register with a social network like Facebook, even though the user is not actually aware of how the social network operator processes the user's personal data. The user may consent to the processing of personal data for advertising purposes, although the user does not know the exact scope of processing. Treating such agreement or consent as legally non-effective, although the user was, or could have been, aware of the lack of complete information, would neglect the self-determination of the individual and the principle of the freedom to contract.

8.4 Contribution of this Work to Development of Theory

This work adds to the legal discussion a detailed analysis based on actual data. While there already exists a body of literature with regard to the specific legal questions that have been discussed in this work, very little of this discussion is based on the actual reception of data protection information. On the other hand, quite a number of studies examine the actual behaviour of data subjects, but without using the results for the legal interpretation of the relevant statutory framework. This work bridges this gap with regard to the selected legal questions.

It may also be noted that the use of quantitative methods for the purpose of legal interpretation seems to be a rather novel and, one might argue, alien concept. It is certainly not without reason that quantitative analysis does not play a relevant role in a hermeneutical field such as law. However, this work shows that

It should also be emphasised that data protection law literature tends to adopt a "data-protection-friendly" approach. To some degree, the authors (and, in particular, the public data protection authorities' publications) fail to sufficiently challenge the underlying assumptions. This work shows that the importance attached to information obligations does not appear to be justified or, at any rate, should not be accepted without reflection. It provides a more balanced approach, which does not only include the interests of individuals, but of data controllers alike.

8.5 Contribution of this Work to Practice

This work may also serve for the practical application of information duties in that it helps data controllers with regard to the drafting of data protection information/privacy policies, in particular when it comes to assessing the necessary level of detail or the specifics of their content.

9 CONCLUSION

The work shows that no overly detailed data protection information is required. Controllers should aim for concise information, possibly using graphical or colour elements. The focus should be on a readable length rather than an extensively detailed text.

Although the information should in principle be provided in the national language of the place where the services associated with the processing are actively offered and directed, the work showed that the data controller is legally not generally required to tailor the data protection information after the language the data subject actually speaks. In terms of accessibility, where privacy information is provided in text form, this will usually satisfy the "accessibility" test.

It could be shown that, timewise, it is sufficient to provide data protection information simultaneously to the actual service in the context of which data is being processed. Where data is not being collected directly from the data subject, it is sufficient to provide the information in cases involving the disclosure to another recipient only when this disclosure actually occurs or when communication with the data subject is envisaged in the course of such communication. A maximum period of one month applies only in the remaining cases. In case of a change of processing purpose, the additional purpose must be notified to the data subject once. Where the information serves as the basis of a consent, it must be provided before or at least at the same time consent is declared.

In principle, the controller may choose the form in which they provide the information. Oral provision is only permissible if requested by the data subject. However, it is normally sufficient for this purpose if the data subject orally requests the controller's activity, which involves a processing operation and thus impliedly also requests the provision of the necessary information orally. Written form encompasses the electronic form (e.g., email) or the presentation on a website.

Although the assumption of self-commitment regarding the legal bases mentioned in the information is to be rejected, controllers are advised to provide all potentially valid legal bases in the data protection information to pre-empt the notion of a self-restriction. For the information on recipients of personal data, it is sufficient for the controller to provide categories of such recipients rather than the actual company names. In most cases, controllers will also be allowed to only provide criteria to determine storage periods rather than the exact storage period for each data category.

The controller has the legal obligation to provide the information under Articles 13 and 14 GDPR. However, they may choose to offer it via a proxy as long as the relevant data subject is eventually provided with the necessary information. In a joint controllership framework, each of the joint controllers must provide the information required under Art. 13/14 GDPR.

The amount of a fine for failing to provide proper information should usually not be very high. Still, the lawmaker should consider abandoning the fine regime in a future revision of the GDPR, given that data subjects may rely on the right to access, which is similarly effective and is subject to potentially high fines.

This work`s analysis calls for of a more balanced approach than proposed by many authors and data protection authorities, which does not only include the interests of individuals, but of data controllers alike.

REFERENCES

AGOF. (2017).*Ddf August 2017 Angebote Ranking Digital.* https://www.agof.de/en/service-downloads/downloadcenter/download-daily-digital-facts/.

Ayres, I., & Schwartz, A. (2014). The No-Reading Problem in Consumer Contract Law. *Stanford Law Review, 66*(3), 545-609. https:// http://digitalcommons.law.yale.edu/.

Bäcker, M. (2018). In J. Kühling & B. Buchner (Eds.), *GDPR/BDSG.* C.H. Beck.

Bäcker, M. (2020). In J. Kühling & B. Buchner (Eds.), *GDPR/BDSG.* C.H. Beck.

Berendt, B., Günther, O., & Spiekermann, S. (2005). Privacy in e-commerce: Stated preferences vs. actual behavior. *Communications of the ACM, 48*(4), 101-106. http://www.researchgate.net/.

Bergmann, M. (2009). Testing privacy awareness. In V. Matyáš, S. Fischer-Hübner, D. Cvrcek, & P. Švenda (Eds.), *The future of identity in the information society.* 237-253. Springer.

Capistrano, E. P. S., & Chen, J. V. (2015). Information privacy policies: The effects of policy characteristics and online experience. *Computer Standards & Interfaces*, *42*, 24-31.

Carlton, A. M. (2018). *The relationship between privacy notice formats and consumer disclosure decisions: A quantitative study* (Dissertation). Northcentral University. https://search.proquest.com/docview/2217800199?pq-origsite=gscholar&fromopenview=true.

Chua, H. N., Herbland, A., Wong, S. F., & Chang, Y. (2017). Compliance to personal data protection principles: A study of how organizations frame privacy policy notices. *Telematics and Informatics*, *34*(4), 157-170.

Dix, A. (2019). In S. Simitis, G. Hornung & I. Spiecker gen. Döhmann (Eds.). *Datenschutzrecht (Data Protection Law)*. Nomos.

Earp, J. B., & Baumer, D. (2003). Innovative web use to learn about consumer behavior and online privacy. *Communications of the ACM*, *46*(4), 81-83. http://www.researchgate.net/.

Elshout, M., Elsen, M., Leenheer, J., Loos, M., & Luzak, J. (2016). *Study on consumers' attitudes towards Terms and Conditions (T&Cs)*. European Commission. https://ec.europa.eu/info/sites/info/files/terms_and_conditions_final_report_en.pdf.

Enforcement Tracker. (n.d.). *GDPR Enforcement Tracker.* Retrieved October 25, 2002, www.enforcementtracker.com.

Ennöckl, D. (2018). In G. Sydow (Ed.). *GDPR*. Nomos.

European Commission. (2016). *Article 29 Data Protection Working Party: Guideline on transparency under Regulation 2016/679.* https://ec.europa.eu/newsroom/just/document.cfm?doc_id=48850.

European Union Agency for Fundamental Rights. (2014). *Handbook on European data protection law.* https://fra.europa.eu/sites/default/files/fra-2014-handbook-data-protection-law-2nd-ed_en.pdf.

Fodor, M., & Brem, A. (2015). Do privacy concerns matter for Millennials? Results from an empirical analysis of Location-Based Services adoption in Germany. *Computers in Human Behavior*, *53*, 344-353.

Franck, L. (2018). In P. Gola (Ed.). *GDPR.* C.H. Beck.

Frenzel, E. (2018). In B. Paal & D. Pauly (Eds.). *GDPR.* C.H. Beck.

Gerlach, J., Buxmann, P., & Dinev, T. (2019). „They're all the same!" Stereotypical thinking and systematic errors in users' privacy-related judgments about online services. *Journal of the Association for Information Systems*, *20*(6), 787-823.

Gluck, J., Schaub, F., Friedman, A., Habib, H., Sadeh, N., Cranor, L. F., & Agarwal, Y. (2016). How short is too short? Implications of length and framing on the effectiveness of privacy notices. In *Twelfth Symposium on Usable Privacy and Security* (pp. 321-340). ACM. https://www.usenix.org/system/files/conference/soups2016/soups2016-paper-gluck.pdf.

Groom, V., & Calo, M.R. (2011). *Reversing the privacy paradox: An experimental study. Stanford.* TPRC. https://papers.ssrn.com/sol3/papers.cfm?abstract_id=1993125.

Heckmann, D. & Paschke, A. (2018). In E. Ehmann & M. Selmayr (Eds.). *GDPR*. C.H. Beck.

Herbst, T. (2018). In J. Kühling & B. Buchner (Eds.), *GDPR/BDSG*. C.H. Beck.

Kamlah, W. (2016). In K.-U. Plath (Ed.). *GDPR*. Dr. Otto Schmidt.

Kelley, P.G., Cesca, L., Bresee, J., & Cranor, L.F. (2010). *Standardizing privacy notices: An online study of the nutrition label approach*. Pittsburgh, https://www.cylab.cmu.edu/_files/pdfs/tech_reports/CMUCyLab09014.pdf.

Kettner, S.E., Thorun, C., & Vetter, M. (2018). *Wege zur besseren Informiertheit - Verhaltenswissenschaftliche Ergebnisse zur Wirksamkeit des One-Pager-Ansatzes und weitere Lösungsansätze im Datenschutz*. Berlin, https://www.conpolicy.de/data/user_upload/Studien/Bericht_ConPolicy_2018_02_Wege_zur_besseren_Informiertheit.pdf.

Kljun, M., Vičič, J., Pucihar, K. Č., & Kavšek, B. (2015,). "I Agree": The Effects of Embedding Terms of Service Key Points in Online User Registration Form. In J. Abascal, S. Barbosa, M. Fetter, T. Gross, P. Palanque, & M. Winckler (Eds.), *IFIP Conference on Human-Computer Interaction* (pp. 420-427). Springer. https://link.springer.com/chapter/10.1007/978-3-319-22668-2_32.

Knyrim, R. (2018). In E. Ehmann & M. Selmayr (Eds.). *GDPR*. C.H. Beck.

Lee, H., Au, N., & Law, R. (2013). Presentation formats of policy statements on hotel websites and privacy concerns: A multimedia learning theory perspective. *Journal of Hospitality & Tourism Research, 37*(4), 470-489.

Levy, A., & Hastak, M. (2008). Consumer comprehension of financial privacy notices. Interagency Notice Project. https://www.ftc.gov/system/files/documents/reports/quantitative-research-levy-hastak-report/quantitative_research_-_levy-hastak_report.pdf.

McDonald, A. M., Reeder, R. W., Kelley, P. G., & Cranor, L. F. (2009). A comparative study of online privacy policies and formats. In I. Goldberg & M. J. Atallah, (Eds.), *International Symposium on Privacy Enhancing Technologies Symposium* (pp. 37-55). Springer.

Nebel, J. U. (2018). The Effectiveness of Privacy Policies and What it Can Mean for the GDPR. In *Enterprise and Competitive Environment: Conference Proceedings*. Brno: Mendelova univerzita v Brně, 2018, p. 453--460. ISBN 978-80-7509-561-9. http://ece.mendelu.cz/wcd/w-rek-ece/ece2018_fin.pdf.

Nebel, J. U. (2019). Information Duties under the GDPR: What Level of Detail Is Required? In HAMPEL, D. *PEFnet 2019: Abstracts*. 1st ed. Brno: Mendelova univerzita v Brně, 2019, p. 95--96. ISBN 978-80-7509-692-0.

Nebel, J. U. (2021). Administrative Fines for Infringement of Information Duties:Aggravating and Mitigating Factors in Light of Data Subjects' Indifference. In European Data Protection Law Review. Berlin. Lexxion, 2021, p. 285--295. DOI: https://doi.org/10.21552/edpl/2021/2/21.

Norberg, P. A., Horne, D. R., & Horne, D. A. (2007). The privacy paradox: Personal information disclosure intentions versus behaviors. *Journal of consumer affairs*, *41*(1), 100-126.

Paal, B. & Hennemann, M. (2018). In B. Paal & D. Pauly (Eds.). *GDPR*. C.H. Beck.

Pan, Y., & Zinkhan, G. M. (2006). Exploring the impact of online privacy disclosures on consumer trust. *Journal of retailing*, *82*(4), 331-338.

Phoenix Strategic Perspectives. (2013). *Survey of Canadians on Privacy-Related Issues*. https://www.priv.gc.ca/media/3323/por_2013_01_e.pdf.

Plaut, V. C., & Bartlett III, R. P. (2012). Blind consent? A social psychological investigation of non-readership of click-through agreements. *Law and human behavior*, *36*(4), 293-311.

Pötters, S. (2017). In P. Gola (Ed.). *GDPR*. C.H. Beck.

Quaas, S. (2017). In H. Wolff & S. Brinck (Eds.). *BeckOK Data Protection Law*. C.H. Beck.

Quaas, S. (2020). In H. Wolff & S. Brinck (Eds.). *BeckOK Data Protection Law*. C.H. Beck.

Quaas, S. (2019). In H. Wolff & S. Brinck (Eds.). *BeckOK Data Protection Law*. C.H. Beck.

Raschke, P., Küpper, A., Drozd, O., & Kirrane, S. (2017, September). Designing a GDPR-compliant and usable privacy dashboard. In M. Hansen, E. Kosta, I. Nai-Fovino, S. Fischer-Hübner (Eds.), *IFIP International Summer School on Privacy and Identity Management* (pp. 221-236). Springer. https://doi.org/10.1007/978-3-319-92925-5_14 (last accessed 19.10.2020).

Reeder, R. W., Kelley, P. G., McDonald, A. M., & Cranor, L. F. (2008, October). A user study of the expandable grid applied to P3P privacy policy visualization. In *Proceedings of the 7th ACM Workshop on Privacy in the Electronic Society* (pp. 45-54). ACM. https://dl.acm.org/doi/pdf/10.1145/1456403.13.

Riesenhuber, K. (Ed.). (2015). *Europäische Methodenlehre: Handbuch für Ausbildung und Praxis* (3rd ed.). Walter de Gruyter.

Schmidt-Wudy, F. (2019). In H. Wolff & S. Brinck (Eds.). *BeckOK Data Protection Law*. C.H. Beck.

Soumelidou, A., & Tsohou, A. (2019). Effects of privacy policy visualization on users' information privacy awareness level: The case of Instagram. *Information Technology & People*, *33*(2), 502-534.

Spanish Data Protection Agency. (2009). *International Standards on the Protection of Personal Data and Privacy*. The Madrid Resolution. https://edps.europa.eu/sites/edp/files/publication/09-11-05_madrid_int_standards_en.pdf.

Spiekermann, S., Grossklags, J., & Berendt, B. (2001, October). E-privacy in 2nd generation E-commerce: privacy preferences versus actual behavior. In Proceedings of the 3rd ACM conference on Electronic Commerce (pp. 38-47). ACM. https://www.csee.umbc.edu/~kolari1/Mining/papers/spiekermann01eprivacy.pdf.

Steinfeld, N. (2016). "I agree to the terms and conditions":(How) do users read privacy policies online? An eye-tracking experiment. *Computers in human behavior*, *55*, 992-1000.

Stotz, R. (2015). In K. Riesenhuber (Ed.). *Europäische Methodenlehre: Handbuch für Ausbildung und Praxis* (3rd ed.). Walter de Gruyter.

Strahilevitz, L. J., & Kugler, M. B. (2016). Is privacy policy language irrelevant to consumers? *The Journal of Legal Studies*, *45*(Suppl. 2), S69-S95.

Vail, M. W., Earp, J. B., & Antón, A. I. (2008). An empirical study of consumer perceptions and comprehension of web site privacy policies. *IEEE Transactions on Engineering Management*, *55*(3), 442-454.

Vu, K. P. L., Chambers, V., Garcia, F. P., Creekmur, B., Sulaitis, J., Nelson, D., ... & Proctor, R. W. (2007, July). How users read and comprehend privacy policies. In *Symposium on Human Interface and the Management of Information* (pp. 802-811). Springer. https://link.springer.com/content/pdf/10.1007/978-3-540-73354-6_88.pdf.

ABOUT THE AUTHOR

Jens Nebel has been one of the frequently recommended lawyers for data protection and IT law in Germany for years. Legal 500 recommends him for IT and digitalization and writes in the current issue: "Outstanding professional quality, astute, meticulous, clear, advises holistically and tactically, thinks quickly and comprehensively about a problem from the client's perspective." In 2024, 2020 and 2018, WirtschaftsWoche named Jens Nebel one of Germany's best IT lawyers. The recognised medium also named him as one of the leading lawyers in data protection law in 2021 and 2022. Handelsblatt and BestLawyers have also consistently listed Jens Nebel as one of the best IT lawyers in Germany since 2019. The nationally published Kanzleimonitor has been recommending Jens Nebel as a "leading lawyer in IT law" ever since 2020. In addition to several academic publications, Jens Nebel regularly comments on data protection and IT law issues in media published throughout Germany, such as the FAZ, Süddeutsche Zeitung or SPIEGEL. He also acted as the defendant in one of the most important data protection proceedings before the European Court of Justice.

www.ingramcontent.com/pod-product-compliance
Lightning Source LLC
LaVergne TN
LVHW022009200926
848481LV00007B/2312
* 9 7 9 8 8 9 6 8 6 2 1 5 4 *